MICROSOFT **Access 97**®

MICROSOFT® CERTIFIED
BLUE RIBBON EDITION

 **ADDISON-WESLEY**

An imprint of Addison Wesley Longman, Inc.

Reading, Massachusetts ▲ Menlo Park, California ▲ New York
Harlow, England ▲ Don Mills, Ontario ▲ Sydney ▲ Mexico City ▲ Madrid ▲ Amsterdam

Acquisitions Editor: *Anita Devine*
Editorial Assistant: *Holly Rioux*
Senior Production Supervisor: *Juliet Silveri*
Copyeditors: *Barbara Conway, Cynthia Benn*
Proofreaders: *Holly McLean-Aldis, Cynthia Benn*
Technical Editors: *Dawn Remmel, Emily Kim*
Indexers: *Mark Kmetzko, Bernice Eisen, Irv Hershman*
Page Checking: *MaryBeth Pitman, Cynthia Benn*
Compositor: *Gillian Hall, The Aardvark Group*
Technical Art Consultant: *Joe Vetere*
Cover Design Supervisor: *Gina Hagen*
Text and cover design: *Linda Wade*
Senior Marketing Manager: *Tom Ziolkowski*
Senior Marketing Coordinator: *Deanna Storey*
Print Buyer: *Sheila Spinney*

ISBN 0-201-44851-3

Addison-Wesley Publishing Company
Jacob Way
Reading, MA   01867
Web: http://hepg.awl.com
Email: is@awl.com

2 3 4 5 6 7 8 9 10-DOW-0099

To Wendy and Michael,
The two most important people in my life

PREFACE

Welcome to the *Microsoft Certified Blue Ribbon Edition of Microsoft Access 97*® by Tim Duffy. This text is approved courseware for the Microsoft Office User Specialist program. After completing the projects in this book, students will be prepared to take the Expert-level exam for Microsoft Access 97®.

Computer literacy is becoming a necessity in a world supercharged with information that is continually evolving and changing. Millions of computers, both individually and in vast networks that span the globe, are constantly processing, analyzing, and organizing information. Advances in hardware and technology that once took decades, then years, now occur with startling frequency.

The challenge is real, it is identifiable, and it is immediate. What does one need to know to achieve and maintain both academic and business success in this technological maelstrom? For more than two decades, Tim Duffy, professor at Illinois State University, and writer, has been answering this question. As a teacher, he has taught introductory computer courses to thousands of his own students; as an author, he has introduced the very same computing concepts and skills to millions of students worldwide through his highly successful series.

In both his classes and his books, Duffy achieves a perfect balance between concept and skill, the why and the how, of computing. The why is the foundation of computing. Learn the concept and why that concept is important, and you can implement any skill. Because he teaches introductory computing throughout the school year, Duffy has intimate knowledge of exactly what conceptual information and what techniques students need and want to learn, and how to present enough of each to interest and challenge these active learners. Duffy knows what works in the classroom and what works in the computer labs. He knows where students can trip up, what assignments will make them think, what examples and exercises will illuminate the concepts, and what techniques will teach.

Duffy teaches what he writes and writes what he teaches. In his books, he brings his classroom teaching experience directly to you with the most innovative, up-to-date material available anywhere. His pedagogy is classroom tried and tested. There are completely new exercises and assignments, an all-new Windows 95-influenced design, and eye-popping graphics for today's visually oriented students. There are Internet and World Wide Web examples and active learning projects. The new Running Case sections are built around everyday problems that require both critical thinking and mastery of specific skills.

BUILDING KNOWLEDGE

For Professor Duffy, learning is like building knowledge. A concept is presented, a feature or task is briefly described, and then students work with it. They complete an exercise or practice a task. Once that task is learned, they add a little more, building on what they are learning. After completing a small group of such tasks, each within its own context, students are presented with projects that unify the concepts and the skills. To achieve this natural balance between concepts and skills, there is constant reinforcement and evaluation throughout the book, including:

- Unifying Features. In the *Microsoft Certified Blue Ribbon Edition of Office 97*® *Professional* and available as a separate module, *Common Features of Microsoft Office 97*® applications are covered first to give students the big picture of how to use an integrated suite.

- Active Learning. **Exercises** apply software commands and features of each Office 97 application program to a specific problem, reinforcing skills described in the text.

- **Running Case**. Everyday problems are presented with just enough information to challenge the students. The Running Case teaches critical thinking while reinforcing the basic skills that students have learned to that point.

- **Document to Web Presentation**. In-depth coverage shows students how to turn an ordinary document into a professional presentation, enhance its appearance, put it on the Web, and then improve the Web page to produce a professional electronic document.

- Task Steps and Reference. **Reinforcing the Exercise** sections provide students with summary information on how a task is performed to reinforce learning and to provide a reference for the future.

- Self-Learning. **On Your Own** boxes allow students to gain additional mastery of features as they explore Office 97 applications on their own.

- **Timely Tips**. Special notations tell students what potential traps they may encounter with a software tool, what can go wrong, and how to remedy the problem.

- **Toolbar Button Reference**. Tables of toolbar buttons give students a central location to find summaries of buttons found on frequently used toolbars.

- **Keyboard and Toolbar Icons**. Task-specific icons appear frequently in headings and tables to help students identify and remember keystrokes or toolbar buttons.

- Self-Evaluation. **End-of-session exercises** offer reinforcement in multiple formats: true/false, multiple choice, short answer, and project-based questions.

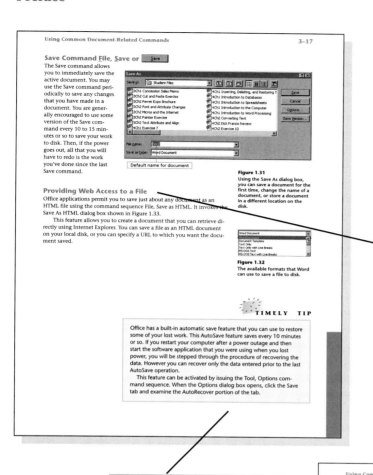

Using Common Document-Related Commands   3–17

Save Command File, Save or [Save]

The Save command allows you to immediately save the active document. You may use the Save command periodically to save any changes that you have made in a document. You are generally encouraged to use some version of the Save command every 10 to 15 minutes or so to save your work to disk. Then, if the power goes out, all that you will have to redo is the work you've done since the last Save command.

Default name for document

Figure 1.31
Using the Save As dialog box, you can save a document for the first time, change the name of a document, or store a document in a different location on the disk.

Providing Web Access to a File

Office applications permit you to save just about any document as an HTML file using the command sequence File, Save as HTML. It invokes the Save As HTML dialog box shown in Figure 1.33.

This feature allows you to create a document that you can retrieve directly using Internet Explorer. You can save a file as an HTML document on your local disk, or you can specify a URL to which you want the document saved.

Figure 1.32
The available formats that Word can use to save a file to disk.

⛅ **TIMELY TIP**

Office has a built-in automatic save feature that you can use to restore some of your lost work. This AutoSave feature saves every 10 minutes or so. If you restart your computer after a power outage and then start the software application that you were using when you lost power, you will be stepped through the procedure of recovering the data. However you can recover only the data entered prior to the last AutoSave operation.

This feature can be activated by issuing the Tool, Options command sequence. When the Options dialog box opens, click the Save tab and examine the AutoRecover portion of the tab.

Duffy takes advantage of the **Web-aware tools** provided with Office 97 to help students translate their skills for use with the Internet and the Web.

Timely Tips inform students of helpful shortcuts, potential mistakes, or troubleshooting measures they can use with the text.

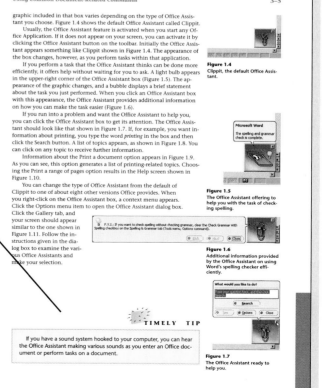

Using Common Document-Related Commands   3–5

graphic included in that box varies depending on the type of Office Assistant you choose. Figure 1.4 shows the default Office Assistant called Clippit.

Usually, the Office Assistant feature is activated when you start any Office Application. If it does not appear on your screen, you can activate it by clicking the Office Assistant button on the toolbar. Initially the Office Assistant appears something like Clippit shown in Figure 1.4. The appearance of the box changes, however, as you perform tasks within that application.

If you perform a task that the Office Assistant thinks can be done more efficiently, it offers help without waiting for you to ask. A light bulb appears in the upper-right corner of the Office Assistant box (Figure 1.5). The appearance of the graphic changes, and a bubble displays a brief statement about the task you just performed. When you click an Office Assistant box with this appearance, the Office Assistant provides additional information on how you can make the task easier (Figure 1.6).

If you run into a problem and want the Office Assistant to help you, you can click the Office Assistant box to get its attention. The Office Assistant should look like that shown in Figure 1.7. If, for example, you want information about printing, you type the word *printing* in the box and then click the Search button. A list of topics appears, as shown in Figure 1.8. You can click on any topic to receive further information.

Information about the Print a document option appears in Figure 1.9. As you can see, this option generates a list of printing-related topics. Choosing the Print a range of pages option results in the Help screen shown in Figure 1.10.

You can change the type of Office Assistant from the default of Clippit to one of about eight other versions Office provides. When you right-click on the Office Assistant box, a context menu appears. Click the Options menu item to open the Office Assistant dialog box. Click the Gallery tab, and your screen should appear similar to the one shown in Figure 1.11. Follow the instructions given in the dialog box to examine the various Office Assistants and make your selection.

Figure 1.4
Clippit, the default Office Assistant.

Figure 1.5
The Office Assistant offering to help you with the task of checking spelling.

Figure 1.6
Additional information provided by the Office Assistant on using Word's spelling checker efficiently.

⛅ **TIMELY TIP**

If you have a sound system hooked to your computer, you can hear the Office Assistant making various sounds as you enter an Office document or perform tasks on a document.

Figure 1.7
The Office Assistant ready to help you.

Shortcut Icons

Check to see if your screen displays shortcut icons like those shown in Figure 1.1. Such shortcut icons may have been placed on your desktop screen by your school computer lab administrator. You can double-click one of these icons to start the application it represents. Notice that shortcut icons have a curved arrow embedded in a square to indicate that they are indeed shortcuts.

Using the Start Button

The menus invoked by clicking the Start button can also be used to start an Office application program. You first click the Start button to activate the Start menu, and then you point to Programs to activate that menu.

The next action you take depends on what appears on the Programs menu. If single application programs are listed, as shown in Figure 1.2, then you can click the desired program and a window will open for that application. If a Microsoft Office option appears on the Programs menu, click that, and then click the desired application when the menu for Office appears.

Figure 1.2
A list of Office-related programs displayed in the Programs menu invoked using the Start, Programs command sequence.

✔ *On Your Own*

Your version of Microsoft Office may include a **shortcut bar** (Figure 1.1), which is a long, narrow bar that appears at the top of the screen. The shortcut bar allows you to quickly access existing documents or create new ones. It also provides direct access to the Schedule+ or Outlook feature (not covered in this text), as well as methods for accessing the Help feature or additional information that might be stored on a CD.

Using an Associated Document

As discussed in Session 2 of the Windows module, you can start an application by double-clicking the icon for an associated document. You can see associated documents when you are viewing the contents of a disk or folder using the My Computer window (Figure 1.3). If the icon for the associated document has an *X*, Excel starts and the document is loaded. If the icon has a *W*, Microsoft Word starts and the document is loaded. (Review Session 2 of the Windows module if you have any questions about other associated document icons.)

USING THE OFFICE ASSISTANT

Every Office application provides help through a feature called the **Office Assistant**. There are several types of Office Assistants available. All appear as a box in the lower-right corner of the screen, and the

Figure 1.3
The 97 Student Files folder window with files shown for the Internet Explorer, Word, Excel, and the Binder.

On Your Own boxes
encourage students to explore the full range of features available in Office 97 applications.

Hands-On Exercises,
based on the Running Case, give step-by-step instructions for learning each application. Numerous screen captures and button icons show students exactly what they need to know.

Figure 1.33
The Save As HTML dialog box allows you to create a file that can be accessed using a Web Browser like Internet Explorer.

Hands-On Exercise: Using File Commands

Isabel wants to examine several of the file-oriented commands that are found in various Office applications.

1. **Start Word.**

   Click to open the Start menu.

   Click to open the Programs menu. If your computer has an Office 97 option, click that option.

   Click to start Word. You should see a screen like that shown in Figure 1.34.

Figure 1.34
The Word application window.

2. **Open two documents using the Open button on the toolbar.**

   Click to open the Open dialog box. Make the necessary changes to access the disk or folder containing the student files used with this textbook.

Figure 1.34
The Word application window.

4. **Verify the number of documents that you have opened.**

Window   Click to display the Window menu (Figure 1.38). You should see the names of the two files you have just loaded as well as the name of the blank document (Document2).

4Ch1 Introduction   Click this document name. You should now see this
to Databases   document displayed in the Word window.

Figure 1.35
The Word window with the 4Ch1 Introduction to Databases document loaded.

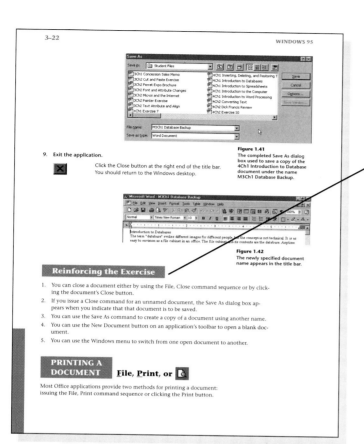

9. Exit the application.

Click the Close button at the right end of the title bar. You should return to the Windows desktop.

Figure 1.41
The completed Save As dialog box used to save a copy of the 4Ch1 Introduction to Database document under the name M3Ch1 Database Backup.

Figure 1.42
The newly specified document name appears in the title bar.

Reinforcing the Exercise

1. You can close a document either by using the File, Close command sequence or by clicking the document's Close button.
2. If you issue a Close command for an unnamed document, the Save As dialog box appears when you indicate that that document is to be saved.
3. You can use the Save As command to create a copy of a document using another name.
4. You can use the New Document button on an application's toolbar to open a blank document.
5. You can use the Windows menu to switch from one open document to another.

PRINTING A DOCUMENT
File, Print, or

Most Office applications provide two methods for printing a document: issuing the File, Print command sequence or clicking the Print button.

Reinforcing the Exercise sections help students recall and refer to the work they have completed.

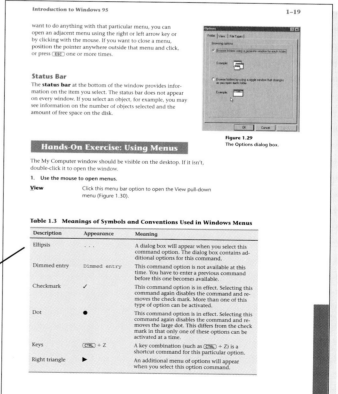

want to do anything with that particular menu, you can open an adjacent menu using the right or left arrow key or by clicking with the mouse. If you want to close a menu, position the pointer anywhere outside that menu and click, or press ESC one or more times.

Status Bar

The **status bar** at the bottom of the window provides information on the item you select. The status bar does not appear on every window. If you select an object, for example, you may see information on the number of objects selected and the amount of free space on the disk.

Figure 1.29
The Options dialog box.

Hands-On Exercise: Using Menus

The My Computer window should be visible on the desktop. If it isn't, double-click it to open the window.

1. Use the mouse to open menus.

View   Click this menu bar option to open the View pull-down menu (Figure 1.30).

Table 1.3 Meanings of Symbols and Conventions Used in Windows Menus

Description	Appearance	Meaning
Ellipsis	. . .	A dialog box will appear when you select this command option. The dialog box contains additional options for this command.
Dimmed entry	Dimmed entry	This command option is not available at this time. You have to enter a previous command before this one becomes available.
Checkmark	✓	This command option is in effect. Selecting this command again disables the command and removes the check mark. More than one of this type of option can be activated.
Dot	●	This command option is in effect. Selecting this command again disables the command and removes the large dot. This differs from the check mark in that only one of these options can be activated at a time.
Keys	CTRL + Z	A key combination (such as CTRL + Z) is a shortcut command for this particular option.
Right triangle	▶	An additional menu of options will appear when you select this option command.

Tables of keyboard or **toolbar icons and symbols** provide students with a quick reference to the conventions and uses of Office 97 applications.

WEB INTEGRATION

The Web site created for this text is **http://hepg.awl.com/office97**. Web-based exercises appear at the end of each session in the Internet Exercises section. The Web site provides an interactive experience for students as they complete exercises in the text that send them to the site for information or files. In the Web exercises, Duffy teaches students how to view and save graphics, how to navigate on the Web, and how to download files; he even offers a guide to buying a personal computer and help on creating personal home pages.

ANCILLARIES

Instructor's Printed Supplements

The printed Instructor's Manual includes a Test Bank and Transparency Masters for each project in the student text. The Test Bank contains tests with answers, and consists of multiple choice, true/false, and fill-in questions that refer to pages in the student text. Transparency Masters illustrate key concepts and screen captures from the text. The Instructor's Manual also offers teaching notes to help integrate current technology (such as the text Web site) into a modern course on Office 97, along with objectives and an outline for each session, and grading tips.

Instructor's Web Site

Instructors get extra support for this text from supplemental materials from our Instructor's password-protected Web site, including screen shots, diagrams, and tables from the text, and files that correspond to key figures in the book that can be used as electronic slides. Screen-by-screen steps in a project can be displayed in class or reviewed by students in the computer lab. The Instructor's Web Site also includes the entire Instructor's Manual with Test Bank in Microsoft® Word format, PowerPoint presentation slides to support classroom lectures for each session (the slides can be printed six per page and distributed to students to facilitate note taking), and a Computerized Test Bank to create printed tests, network tests, and self-assessment quizzes for the Internet. Student data files and completed data files are available. All electronic files can be downloaded from the Instructor's Web site at http://hepg.awl.com/office97. Contact your Addison Wesley Longman Sales Representative for your ID and password.

Student Supplements

QWIZ Assessment Software is a network-based skills assessment-testing program that measures student proficiency with Windows 95, Word 97, Excel 97, Access 97, and PowerPoint 97. Professors select the tasks to be tested and get student results immediately. The test is taken in a simulated software environment. On-screen instructions require students to perform tasks just as though they were using the actual application. The program automatically records responses, assesses student accuracy, and reports the resulting score in a printout or disk file as well as to the instructor's gradebook. The students receive immediate feedback from the program, including learning why a particular task was scored as incorrect and what part of the lab manual to review.

TECHSUITE PROGRAM

The Duffy Office 97 applications texts are available separately or in a single *Microsoft Certified Blue Ribbon Edition of Office 97® Professional* volume. The Office 97 Professional suite includes Common Features of Office 97, Windows 95 with Active Desktop and Windows 98, Internet Explorer 4, Word 97, Excel 97, Access 97, and PowerPoint 97.

In addition to the Duffy *Microsoft Certified Blue Ribbon Edition of Office 97® Professional* lab series, Addison Wesley also offers dozens of proven and class-tested lab manuals within the *SELECT Lab Series*; from the latest operating systems and browsers to the most popular application software for word processing, spreadsheets, databases, presentation graphics, and integrated packages to HTML and programming. Knowing that you have specific needs for your lab course, we offer the quick and affordable custom TechSuite program. Lab Manuals from the *SELECT Lab Series* can be packaged with any of the Duffy Office 97 Professional lab books. Many of the *SELECT Lab Series* are available in *Brief, Standard,* or *PLUS* Editions that best suit your classroom needs. Your choice of lab manuals will be sent to the bookstore in a TechSuite box, allowing students to purchase all books in one convenient package at a significant discount.

In addition, your school may qualify for Office 97 upgrades or licenses. Your Addison Wesley Longman representative will be happy to work with you and your bookstore manager to provide the most current menu of application software. Your representative will also outline the ordering process, and provide pricing, ISBNs, and delivery information. Call 1-800-447-2226 or visit our Web site at http://hepg.awl.com and click on ordering information.

ACKNOWLEDGMENTS

I am amazed that fifteen years have passed since I started the first edition of Four Software Tools. At that time, I was totally unaware of the time-consuming efforts needed to produce a college-level textbook. Since then, however, I have developed a sincere appreciation of what is required to make a successful text. The success formula includes family, friends, colleagues, and many individuals in the publishing business. I remain deeply indebted to my wife, Wendy, who encouraged me to write the original version of Four Software Tools. Without her encouragement, the original text would never have been finished, and without her continued support, these projects would be impossible to accomplish.

I also want to express my sincere appreciation to the reviewers of this manuscript:

Jill Betts, Tyler Junior College
Bill Daley, University of Oregon
Kathryn A. Drexel, Drexel Associates
Peter Drexel, Plymouth State College
Seth Hock, Columbus State Community College
Marie McCooey, Bryant College
Vincent J. Motto, Asnuntuck Community-Technical College
Stephen C. Solosky, Nassau Community College
Melinda C. White, Santa Fe Community College

Individuals at the publishing company also play an important role. Addison Wesley Longman's editorial staff is superb. With warm feelings, I would like to acknowledge Anita Devine and Ed Moura. Maureen Allaire initially signed this book and over the years has had much to do with many of my books. I am pleased to be working with Anita Devine, who brings a wealth of editorial experience in microcomputer texts. Ed Moura, Editor-in-Chief, brought a number of excellent ideas to this project. Holly Rioux, editorial assistant, made certain that everything was going on an even keel. Juliet Silveri, Jennifer Pelland, Bess Deck, Sue Purdy Pelosi and Barbara Conway made the publishing process smooth and professional. Emily Kim's and Cynthia Benn's technical edits and copyedits helped to assure internal consistency of the textbooks.

An often-overlooked ingredient in the success of textbooks is the publisher's marketing and sales staff. Tom Ziolkowski's experienced efforts in developing a marketing plan are greatly appreciated. I am convinced that the Addison Wesley Longman sales staff is one of the best in the business.

A dedication is not complete without including my son, Michael. Michael continues to make any writing project a challenge. His requests to go biking, swimming, or pursue a new interest are much appreciated. Michael especially likes to surf the Web to complete homework assignments and has become a ten-year-old master at ferreting out information from the Web.

CONTENTS

Microsoft Access 97 for Windows

Introduction to Databases and Access 97

After completing this session, you should be able to:

➤ List some of the basic concepts of a database

➤ Use Access 97 menus

➤ Know the parts of the Access window

➤ Issue Access commands

➤ Create a table structure

➤ Add and edit data in a table

Isabel has received a request from Alice, the manager of the health club at the Sports Center Civic Arena, for help in developing an Access database to keep track of membership for the health club. This information is currently contained in an index card file.

In addition to the membership application, Isabel and Alice also want to be able to provide members with the ability to have an internal line of credit for the Sports Shop that is part of the Civic Arena. Members will be able to show their active membership cards, and any purchases that they make will automatically be added to their accounts.

INTRODUCTION TO DATABASES

The concept behind a database is simple: A database is like a file cabinet. Just as a file cabinet stores information, so does a database. Just as the folders in a file cabinet are arranged to hold data in some useful order, so are the records in a database. Searching a database for certain information is like searching in a file cabinet. Just as you can change the order of the folders in a file cabinet to suit your convenience, you can also change the order of things in a database.

Database Terminology

A **database** is a set of information related to a specific application. In the context of Access, a database can be viewed as a large repository (like a file cabinet) in which tables, reports, queries, and other objects are stored. When Access creates a database, it places all application-related objects in a file with the .mdb filename extension.

A **table** is the storage entity for a database. It is made up of records that contain data about a single thing, such as a person or a sales transaction.

A **record** is a unit within the table. Each record in a table contains related information about an entity. An entity can be the details of a single business transaction, all of the summary payroll data related to a single employee, or a single customer's name and address and accumulated sales history.

A **field** is a smaller unit within a record that contains a fact about the entity. In a customer record, for instance, one field might contain a customer's last name; another field might contain his or her street address.

A **relational database** allows you to link records from two or more tables based on the contents of a common field.

You can use information from one or more fields to define **keys,** which you use to order, identify, and retrieve the records in the database. Typically you will use more than one key. The **primary key** is the unique identifier for a particular record, most often a customer number or Social Security number. When a database is in primary-key order, the records may appear in the table in order by the contents of the field used to build the primary key, but no two records can have the same key value. You can also define a **secondary key** by information from one or more other fields within the database. You use this key to arrange the database in some other order. For instance, a user might create a secondary key from the first and last name fields. A secondary key differs from a primary key in that it allows multiple occurrences of the same value.

The **table structure** is a set of instructions regarding the arrangement of information within each record, the type of characters (numeric or alphanumeric, for example) used to store each field, and the number of characters required by each field. Once you have structured the table, you can manage it, and you can instruct the computer to do such things as add new records, change existing records, sort and arrange records in a new order, search for and retrieve specific types of records, print data, and delete data.

Designing Fields

It is very important to remember two things when designing the database fields. First, fields should isolate those pieces of data that you may need to use as keys to sort and rearrange records. Second, whereas humans can often identify separate pieces of information within a field, computers generally cannot. For instance, consider the following four lines of customer address information:

> Gerald B. Dixon
> 1526 N. Main
> Bloomington, IL 61704
> (309) 367-8934

How many fields should it take to store these lines in a record? It is possible to store the customer's name in one field. However, this way it would be impossible for the computer to sort records by last name, because it wouldn't know that Gerald is a first name and Dixon a last name. Nor could the computer readily distinguish an address from a telephone number. Thus designers and users of database tables must take care to lay out fields and enter data in rigid, predictable patterns. The computer can then process information in the table solely on the basis of what field the information is in, without any understanding of the meaning of the data. In practice, the above customer information requires eight fields:

First Name	Address	Zip
Middle Initial	City	Phone
Last Name	State	

The name is divided into three fields so records can be sorted by last name and the first name can be used independently of the middle initial. Divisions in the address line let you rearrange records within the database by city, state, or zip code.

Well-designed records provide great flexibility when you choose secondary keys. With the preceding fields, for instance, to produce a report in order by customer name, you could create a key based on first and last names. By changing the keys to last name and city or state, you could produce another report in order by customer name and location.

INTRODUCTION TO ACCESS 97

The Access package is one of the best-selling relational database packages for Windows on the market. Microsoft estimates that currently 10 million people use this database package.

Access 97 Modes

Access provides two different modes. The first is an easy-to-use **menu-driven** interface that lets you issue commands without an in-depth understanding of Access. **Program mode** lets you store instructions in a Visual Basic program file and execute all of them with one command. This book concentrates on using Access from the menu.

Starting Access 97

You can start Access in one of the following two ways:

- If visible, double-click the Microsoft Access shortcut icon.
- Click the Start button; select Programs; if it is visible, click the Office95 entry; and then click the Microsoft Access icon.

The Access Window

Once you have started Access for Windows, a copyright screen briefly appears, showing who purchased the package, the company at which this person works, and the version number of the package. This screen disappears after a few seconds, and the Access window is displayed, along with a dialog box prompting you about which database file to open (Figure 1.1).

Your Access window may not look exactly like Figure 1.1. You may, for instance, have to click the Maximize button to get the window to occupy the entire screen.

The opening dialog box allows you to create a database or open an existing database. While you are using this text to study Access, you will be using two databases: Membership and Projects.

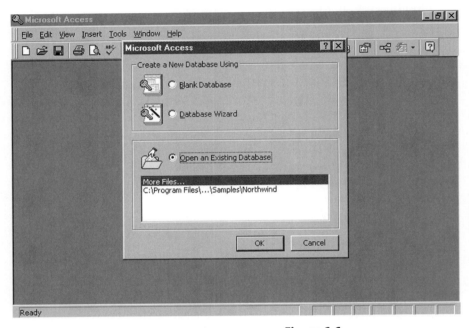

Figure 1.1
The Access window with the opening dialog box.

Title Bar

The title bar (Figure 1.2) indicates that you are in Microsoft Access. The Minimize, Maximize or Restore, and Close buttons are also part of the title bar.

Figure 1.2
The Access title bar.

TIMELY TIP

After you have begun using Access, you can save some time by looking at the files listed in the box under the Open an Existing Database option. If you see the name of the file that you want (you have to have worked on it recently), you simply double-click that filename to open that database.

Menu Bar

Beneath the title bar is the menu bar (Figure 1.3), which contains menu options that activate pull-down menus. The menu options and menus displayed follow standard Windows conventions.

File Edit View Insert Tools Window Help

Figure 1.3
The Access menu bar.

Toolbar

The toolbar (Figure 1.4) contains buttons that you can click to issue commands, instead of using the menu structure. The toolbar buttons vary with the Access features that are active. Table 1.1 shows and describes the most common toolbar buttons.

Figure 1.4
The Access toolbar buttons.

Table 1.1 Toolbar Buttons

Button	Button Name	Purpose
	New Database	Opens a pop-up window from which you can choose a new database to create
	Open Database	Displays the Open dialog box, which you use to activate a database
	Save	Saves the open database
	Print	Prints the active document
	Print Preview	Shows how a report, form, datasheet, or module will appear when printed
	Spelling	Invokes the spelling checker
	Cut	Cuts selected text/data and moves it to the clipboard
	Copy	Copies selected text/data to the clipboard
	Paste	Pastes the contents of the clipboard at the cursor location
	Format Painter	Copies formatting from one object to another
	Undo	Undoes your most recent reversible action
	OfficeLinks	Starts the Microsoft Word Merge Wizard, which allows you to create letters or mailing labels
	Analyze	Starts the Table Analyzer Wizard, which analyzes a table, and if necessary, splits it into related tables and creates a more efficient table design

Table 1.1 Continued

Button	Button Name	Purpose
	Large Icons	Uses large icons for database objects
	Small Icons	Uses small icons for database objects
	List	Uses small icons for database objects to list vertically
	Details	Lists the database name, description, last date modified, date created, type, and owner
	Code	Displays a Visual Basic form module or report module where you can view, edit, create, or run procedures
	Properties	Displays the general properties of the selected object
	Relationships	Allows you to view or edit existing relationships or to define new ones between tables and queries
	New Object	Automatically creates a form based on the selected table or query
	Office Assistant	Opens the Office Assistant to provide you with help

Context Menus

Access 97 makes use of context menus, which are pop-up menus that appear when you right-click particular objects throughout the program. You can use these menus to perform certain operations quickly. For example, if you right-click a table name, the context menu shown in Figure 1.5 appears on-screen.

Database Window

The **Database window** shows all of the tables that are related to the activated database. Each tab along the top represents a different type of object related to the open database.

Status Bar

The status bar appears at the bottom of the screen (Figure 1.6). It displays helpful information while you are using Access. The squares that appear at the right end of the status bar are indicators for such things as the NUM LOCK and CAPS LOCK keys.

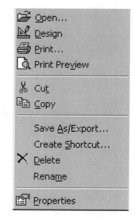

Figure 1.5
The context menu for a table.

Figure 1.6
The Access status bar.

Hands-On Exercise: Opening a Database

Isabel and Alice want to start working with the Membership database.

1. **Start Access.**

2. **Open your copy of the Membership database.**

Open an Existing Database

If necessary, click this option in the opening dialog box.

Click to invoke the Open dialog box. Make the necessary changes to get to the location where your student data files are stored. The Open dialog box should look like Figure 1.7.

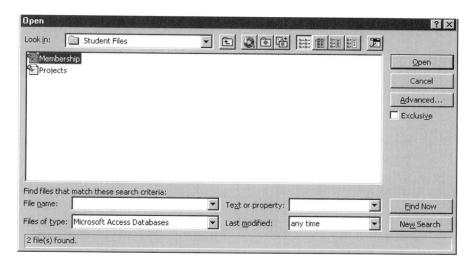

Figure 1.7
The two databases associated with this textbook appear in the Open dialog box.

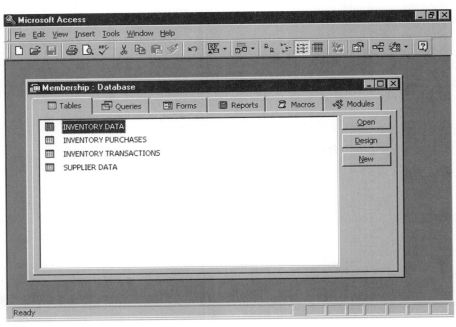

Figure 1.8
The open Membership Database window with the Tables tab activated, containing the databases you will use in this text.

 Double-click this entry to open the Membership database. Your Membership Database window appears as shown in Figure 1.8. By default, the Tables tab is open, displaying the various tables that you will use in this text along with the table you will build in this session.

Reinforcing the Exercise

1. When you start Access, the Access window includes an opening dialog box that you can use to create a new database or open an existing database.

2. Databases that you have worked on recently are listed in a box at the bottom of the opening dialog box.

3. You can open a database quickly by double-clicking a filename that is listed in the opening dialog box.

4. When you open a database, it appears in a Database window, which has tabs that relate to various objects within that database.

Exiting Access   File, Exit or

At the end of an Access session, you must properly exit to Windows either by using the File, Exit command sequence or by clicking the Close button of the Access title bar. If you do not, you may lose data or corrupt files.

CREATING A DATABASE

As mentioned previously, an Access database includes tables that you create. It also includes anything you create related to a table, such as queries and reports (which you will learn about later in the module). A database can track all objects that are related to a specific application. For example, you can store all reports, queries, or forms related to a payroll application in a database called Payroll, and you can store all objects related to a personnel application in a database called Personnel.

To create a database, you first issue the File, New Database command sequence. You then specify the name of the database (the default is db1.mdb) and the location, if it is different from the current location specified in the directories and drive boxes of the New Database dialog box.

CREATING A TABLE STRUCTURE

To create an Access database table, you must first define the table structure, which includes the table name and information about its data fields (name, data type, and length). Once you have created the table structure, you can enter data in the table and manipulate the data.

Naming a Table

Access allows you to use up to 64 characters in table and field names. These characters can include letters, numbers, spaces, and special characters, except the period (.), exclamation mark (!), backquote (`), and brackets ({}). You are also prohibited from using leading spaces and control characters. Do not give a table a filename extension.

Defining Field Types

The **data type** to be stored in a field determines the type of the field: Text, Number, Yes/No, Memo, Date/Time, Currency, AutoNumber, and OLE object.

*   A **Text field** holds any alphanumeric character (number, letter, or special character).

*   A **Number field** is restricted to the plus or minus sign (+ or −), numerals, and the decimal point (.); the decimal point must be counted as part of the field length. Use this data type anytime you want to perform calculations that involve the contents of the field.

*   A **Yes/No field** contains Y (yes) or N (no) and is thus always only one position in length. A yes is stored as a −1, whereas a no is stored as a 0.

*   A **Memo field** holds large documents (up to 64,000 bytes or characters of data). Use Memo fields when you want to store narrative or descriptive information. For instance, you might want to make annotations about a customer's hobbies, children's names, likes and dislikes, and so forth.

*   A **Date/Time field** contains eight positions and automatically has the slashes (/) in the correct locations; an empty Date field appears as _/_/_ .

*   A **Currency field** holds money-related data to be used in calculations. It does a better job of rounding for dollars and cents than a number field. Once you have specified the Currency data type, you usually have to define how the data is to be displayed and stored.

- An **AutoNumber field** allows you to number the records as they appear in a table, query, and so forth. This type of field cannot be updated.

- An **OLE object field** stores objects from other Windows applications that support object linking and embedding (OLE). When you display a record that contains an OLE field, you can view the OLE object (graphic image, graph, worksheet, and so forth) by double-clicking the field. Windows then launches the parent application for the OLE object.

The Membership database will consist of the following fields in each data record:

Membership ID Number	State
Salutation	Zip
First Name	Phone
Middle Initial	Membership Amount
Last Name	Membership Expiration Date
Address	Amount Due
City	Comments

The Membership ID Number field will act as a unique identifier for each record. The Salutation field will be used for generating written correspondence, if necessary, with the customer. The Comments field will contain any information that might be pertinent for each customer (such as likes and dislikes, favorite merchandise, birthdays of children). The Amount Due field will be used to track credit purchases at the gift shop.

You also must decide which type of data is to be stored in each field and how long each field should be. Text data is used for most fields. Why would you want to use text data for the Zip field when a zip code is numeric digits? A common rule of thumb is to store data as text data unless it is to be used in calculations.

The Phone field is also text data because the area code appears between parentheses, and a hyphen appears between the exchange and the number in that exchange. The Membership Amount and Amount Due fields have two positions to the right of the decimal point. The Membership Expiration Date is a Date field, and the Comments field is a Memo field. Table 1.2 shows the breakdown of field names, data types, and field sizes.

It is important not to use too many fields in a record or to define fields that are too large to hold the data. The size of the fields determines how much space they will take on disk. Unused field positions are filled with blanks. Reserving too much room for a field wastes disk storage space.

Setting Field Properties

Besides giving the field name and data type when you are defining the fields of a record, you also want to determine the optimal field length as well as possibly control how the data is to be entered. Field length, alignment, fill characters, color, and other features are controlled via the **Field Properties box** for each field (Figure 1.9).

Table 1.2 Membership Database Fields

Field Name	Data Type	Field Size
MEMBER ID NUMBER	Text	5
SALUTATION	Text	5
FIRST NAME	Text	10
MIDDLE INITIAL	Text	1
LAST NAME	Text	12
ADDRESS	Text	25
CITY	Text	15
STATE	Text	2
ZIP	Text	10
PHONE	Text	13
MEMBERSHIP AMOUNT	Currency	
MEMBERSHIP EXPIRATION DATE	Date/Time	
AMOUNT DUE	Currency	
COMMENTS	Memo	

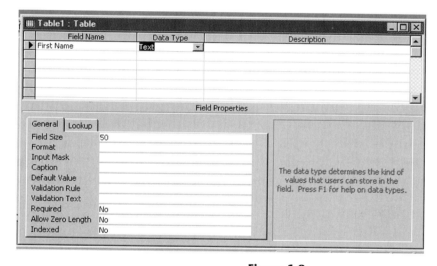

Figure 1.9
The Field Properties box appears after you have defined a field.

Hands-On Exercise: Defining the Table Structure

Isabel and Alice are now going to define the Membership Data table.

1. **If necessary open the Membership database.**

2. **Start the table structure definition process.**

> New
>
> Click to open the New Table dialog box (Figure 1.10). This dialog box determines how you will define the new table.

Design View   Double-click to open the table design win-
                      dow shown in Figure 1.11.

3. **Define the first field.**

                      Click to maximize the table design window.

Type: **MEMBERSHIP ID NUMBER**

Click   Click the first box in the Field Name column.

TAB   Press to accept the text default data type.

Drag   Click and drag to select the 50 in the Field Size cell of the
                      Field Properties box. The 50 should now be in reverse
                      video.

Figure 1.10
The New Table dialog box.

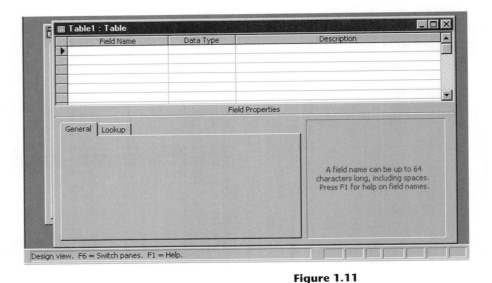

Figure 1.11
**The table design window allows
you to enter the structure of the
new table.**

Type a new field width: **5**

Click   Click the Data Type field in the table design window.

                      Click this button on the table design window toolbar to
                      designate this field as the primary key field.

4. **Enter the second field.**

Click   Click the next row in the Field Name field.

Type: **SALUTATION**

TAB   Press to accept the Text default data type. For a field con-
                      taining another data type, you must click the down arrow
                      to open the Data Type list box (Figure 1.12), and then
                      click the appropriate data type.

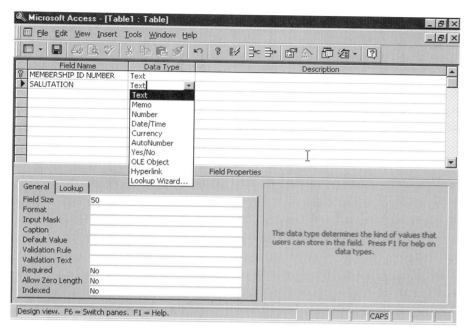

Figure 1.12
The Data Type list box.

Double-click	Double-click to select the 50 in the Field Size cell of the Field Properties box.

Type a new field width: **5**

Click	Click the next row in the Field Name field in the table definition area.

5. **Continue entering the field definitions, using Table 1.2 as a guide.** When you are finished, the structure should look like Figures 1.13 and 1.14. The cursor will be in the Comments field.

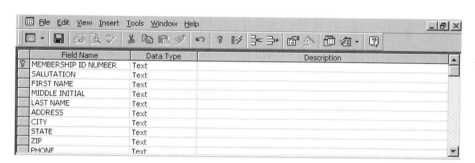

Figure 1.13
The first part of the defined table.

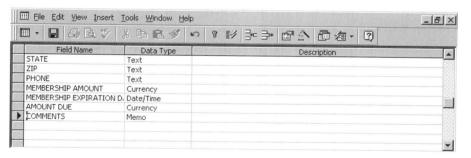

Figure 1.14
The remaining portion of the defined table.

TIMELY TIP

Access provides several ways to make corrections in a table structure:

- Correcting errors is a straightforward process. Use the arrow keys to move to the correct line, (TAB) and (SHIFT) + (TAB) to move the cursor horizontally to the desired field, and then reenter the data.
- If you inadvertently forget to enter a field, position the cursor beneath the field's desired location, and click the Insert Row button on the toolbar of the table design window.

6. Save the table structure.

 Click this button on the toolbar to open the Save As dialog box (Figure 1.15). By default, the table is named Table1.

Type the name of the table: **MEMBERSHIP DATA**

 Click to save the structure to disk and close the dialog box.

 Click this button at the right end of the table design window menu bar.

 Click the Close button of the table design window. You are now returned to the Membership Database window (Figure 1.16). The Membership Data table name appears on the list displayed on the Tables tab.

Figure 1.15
The Save As dialog box.

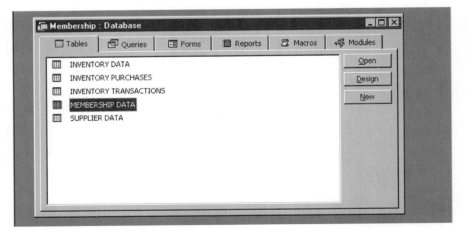

Figure 1.16
The Database window with the newly defined Membership Data table listed.

Reinforcing the Exercise

1. Plan the contents of a table before you define it.
2. Place each piece of data in a separate field.
3. Unless an item containing numbers is to be used for performing calculations, it is typically defined as text data.
4. Properties such as field size and format are defined in the Field Properties box.
5. The unique identifier for a table record is the primary key.

ADDING AND DISPLAYING TABLE DATA

When you double-click a table listed in the Database window, the **Datasheet window** opens. You use the Datasheet window to display a table for which you have created a structure and to add or edit data in a table. For a newly designed table, such as the Membership Data table you just created, the Datasheet window appears as shown in Figure 1.17.

At the top of the Datasheet window is the title bar, which displays the name of the table and the Minimize, Maximize or Restore, and Close buttons. Just below the title bar are the field names for each field you defined in the table structure. Under the field names is the first record of the table; in this case, the record is empty and the pointer is positioned in the first field so you can begin entering data.

At the bottom of the Datasheet window is the **speedbar,** which contains several navigation buttons and displays the record in which the pointer is currently located and the number of records in the entire table. At the right end of the speedbar is a scroll bar you can use to move quickly from field to field.

As you add data to a record, you press (ENTER) when you complete a field to advance to the next field. When you complete the last field in a table and press (ENTER), a new blank record appears.

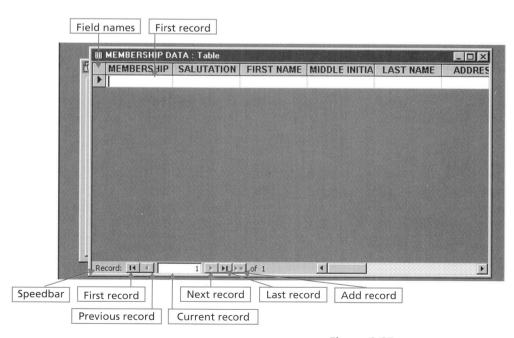

Figure 1.17
The Datasheet window for the Membership Data table.

Hands-On Exercise: Entering Data in a Table

Isabel and Alice need to enter the first records in the Membership database.

1. **Open the Membership database if necessary.**

2. **Open the Datasheet window for the Membership data table.**

MEMBERSHIP DATA Double-click this table name from the list in the Database window. The Datasheet window appears as shown in Figure 1.17.

3. **Maximize the screen.**

  Click to maximize the Datasheet window (Figure 1.18).

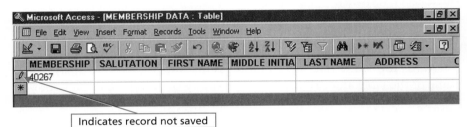

Indicates record not saved

Figure 1.18
The pencil indicates that this record has not been saved to disk.

4. **Enter the first record, using the following as a guide.** (Do not enter information in the Comments field.)

Membership ID Number	Salutation	First Name	Middle Initial	Last Name	Address	City
40267	Mr.	Gerald	I	McDermott	1225 W. Market	Bloomington

State	Zip	Phone	Membership Amount	Membership Expiration	Amount Owed	Comments
IL	61701	(309)662-1257	195.00	12/12/97	250.00	

Notice that as you enter information in the Membership ID Number field, a pencil appears to the left of the record (Figure 1.18). This indicates that this record has not been saved. As you continue to enter information, Access automatically moves everything to the right to display any blank fields.

TIMELY TIP

> When you enter numeric information, Access automatically right-justifies the digits in the field when you press (ENTER). If the number does not have decimal positions, do not enter a decimal point; Access automatically places a decimal point in the appropriate location.

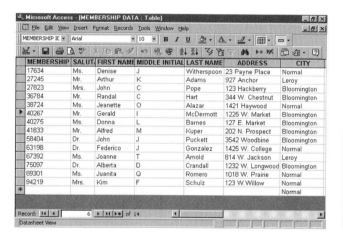

Figure 1.19
The first record of the Membership Data table.

5. **Complete the first record and move to the next record.**

(ENTER)   Press to move to the next record. The asterisk appears next to the first record, indicating Access has automatically saved it to disk. The Datasheet window should look like Figure 1.19. Notice that the record number displayed at the bottom of the window has changed.

6. **Finish entering all 14 records, using Figures 1.20 and 1.21 as guides.**
The pencil icon does not appear in the left margin of the datasheet. As you enter the records, they appear in primary key order

     Click this button of the Datasheet window (on the menu bar).

     Click to close the Datasheet window.

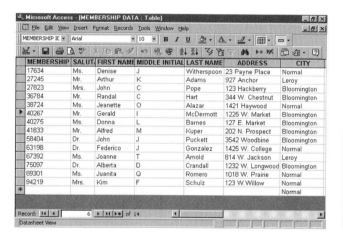

Figure 1.20
The first 7 fields of the first 15 records of the Membership Data table. Don't enter the McDermott record twice. Your field sizes will be larger.

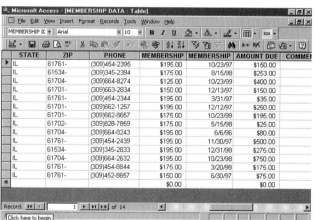

Figure 1.21
The remaining 8 fields of the first 15 records in the Membership Data table.

Reinforcing the Exercise

1. You use the Datasheet window to enter records in a table.
2. Records occupy rows in the datasheet, and fields are in columns.
3. A pencil occurs in the left margin of a record that has not yet been saved.
4. The number of the record appears in the speed bar at the bottom of the Datasheet window.
5. When you press (ENTER) at the end of the last field, a new blank record is added to the datasheet.

    If you note errors in a record, you can correct them using standard editing conventions. A record is saved to the table when you close the Datasheet window or any time you press (PGUP) or (PGDN) as you are entering data. You can also use these keys to view the records in the table to ensure that there are no errors.

OPENING A TABLE

You have now created the Membership Data table and entered 14 records in it. As long as you are still in Access and have not activated any other table, you can double-click the Membership Data table name in the Database window to open the table.

If you quit Access and later want to add records to the Membership Data table, you must reenter Access, open the Membership database, and then open the Membership Data table from the Database window.

TIMELY   TIP

If you somehow close the Datasheet window by mistake and return to the Database window, you can simply double-click the Membership Data table to reopen the Datasheet window.

Once you have activated a table and the Datasheet window is onscreen, you can look at the structure of the table by clicking the Table View button on the toolbar. Once you have obtained the information you needed, click the Datasheet View icon to return to the Datasheet window.

ADDING RECORDS TO A TABLE

You can add records to a table in the Datasheet window, using the same steps you used in the previous Hands-On Exercise. Table 1.3 describes a number of cursor-movement commands for moving within a table and within a screen.

Table 1.3 Cursor-Movement Commands for a Table

Key(s) or Button	Cursor Position
Click the First Record button of the datasheet speedbar	First record
Click the Last Record button of the datasheet speedbar	Last record
HOME	First column
END	Last column
TAB or ENTER	Next column
SHIFT + TAB	Previous column
↑ or ◄ on datasheet speedbar	Previous record
↓ or ► on datasheet speedbar	Next record
CTRL + HOME or ◄|	First record, first column
CTRL + END	Last record, last column
PGUP	Up 26 rows
PGDN	Down 26 rows

Hands-On Exercise: Adding Records to a Table

Isabel and Alice now want to add a record to the Membership Data table.

1. **Start Access if necessary, and then open the Membership Data table.**

MEMBERSHIP DATA   Click this name in the Tables tab of the Database window.

2. **Click the first field in the row that has an asterisk (*) in the left-hand border.** When you have finished adding the new record, return to the database window.

3. **Add a record to the Membership Data table, using Figures 1.22 and 1.23 as guides.** The records will be in order by Membership ID Number, the primary key.

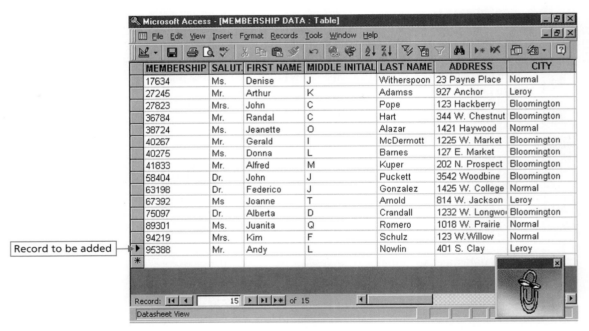

Figure 1.22
The first seven fields of the completed Membership Data table.

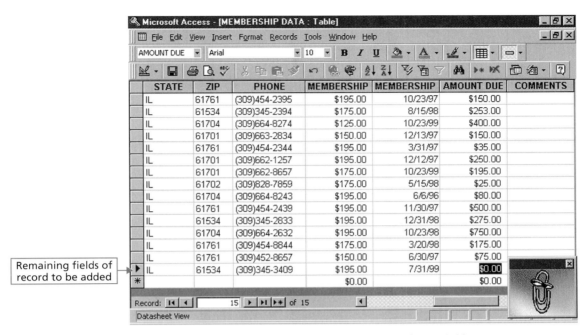

Figure 1.23
The remaining fields of the completed Membership Data table.

Reinforcing the Exercise

1. Before you add records to a table, you must open both the database and the table.
2. Records are displayed in the datasheet in order by the primary key.
3. There are a number of commands that can be used to move around a datasheet displaying table information.

EDITING RECORDS IN A TABLE

Access has a number of commands that you can use for editing text within a field of data. These commands are summarized in Table 1.4.

Table 1.4   Field Editing Commands

Key(s)	Task Performed
F2	Switch from navigation mode to edit mode when using the cursor-movement keys to move among fields and records.
→	Move right one character.
←	Move left one character.
CTRL + →	Move right one word.
CTRL + ←	Move left one word.
HOME	Move to the beginning of the field.
END	Move to the end of the field.
CTRL + END	Move to the end of a multiple line field.
CTRL + HOME	Move to the beginning of a multiple line field.
CTRL + C	Copy to the clipboard.
CTRL + V	Paste contents of clipboard at the insertion point.
CTRL + X	Cut and copy to the clipboard.

Hands-On Exercise: Editing a Field

The Membership Data table now has 15 records. Alice and Isabel examine each record for errors and notice that in record 2 (Figure 1.22) the last name is spelled incorrectly (there should be only one *s*).

1. **If necessary, open the Membership database and the Membership Data table.**

2. **Correct the error.**

              Click to enlarge Datasheet window.

    Adamss   Click to position the cursor to the right of the second *s*.

    BACKSPACE   Press once to delete the second *s*.

3. **Resize the Datasheet window and then close the table.**

              Click to restore the Datasheet window to its original size.

              Click to close the Datasheet window.

> If you want to delete or replace the contents of a cell rather than just change it, use the cursor-movement keys to position the cursor in the field (it should be in reverse video), and then press (DEL). The current contents disappear. To replace the contents of a field, move to that field (the contents is in reverse video). Any data that you enter replaces the highlighted data in the field.

Entering Data in a Memo Field

The Membership Data table has a structure that includes a Comments field with a data type of Memo. None of the records has yet used this field.

Suppose you want to add information to the Comments field in Joanne Arnold's record. You must first position the cursor in the correct row using the appropriate cursor-movement command and then move to the Comments field. You then open the text editor for a Memo field by issuing the Zoom command, (SHIFT) + (F2).

Hands-On Exercise: Entering Data in a Memo Field

Alice wants to add a memo to a record in the table.

1. **Activate the Membership Data table if necessary.**

MEMBERSHIP DATA   Double-click the table listed in the Tables tab of the Database window.

2. **Make an entry in a Memo field.**

(↓)   Press several times to move to the 11th record.

(END)   Press to move to the Comments field.

(SHIFT) + (F2)   Press to issue the Zoom command. The Zoom dialog box shown in Figure 1.24 appears.

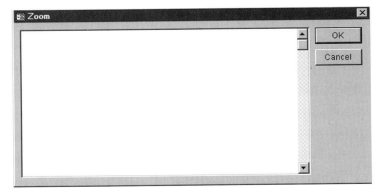

Figure 1.24
The Zoom dialog box for entering a memo.

Type the following in the Zoom window: **Joanne has several hobbies. One that is of special interest is bicycling. Over the past few years, she has won several regional races. She also enjoys driving sports cars. At this time she owns a Mitsubishi Eclipse convertible.**

The screen should look like Figure 1.25.

| OK | Click to save the text to the Comments field.

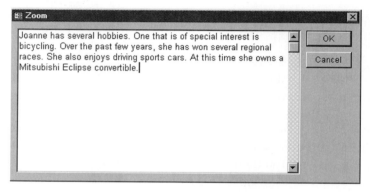

Figure 1.25
The completed dialog box for inserting a memo notation in Joanne's record.

PRINTING A REPORT

Access allows you to quickly generate a printout of records in a table by using the Print button on the toolbar. The printout is called a **report.** You can see how the report will look before you print it by clicking the Print Preview button.

The report starts at the beginning of the table and lists all records. For readability, Access lists the field names above the data and continues printing records. It displays the field names as the first line of the report. If a line is too long, it is printed on the second sheet of paper. All fields are surrounded by a grid.

As Access prints the report, it places the name of the table and the date at the top of each page. It places a page number at the bottom of each page.

Hands-On Exercise: Printing a Report of a Table

Now that they have filled in the Membership Data table, Alice and Isabel would like to print it.

1. **Preview the report.**

Click this button on the toolbar to see what the report will look like when you print it (Figure 1.26). Since the report is so wide, it extends over three pages. Figure 1.26 shows how the first page of the report will print.

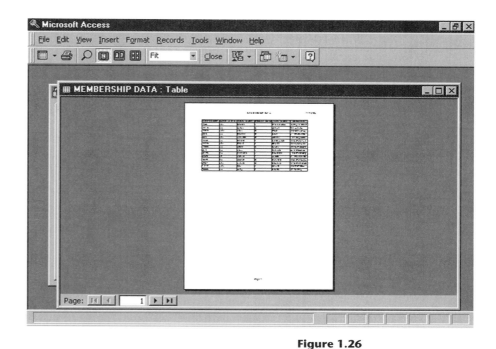

Figure 1.26
The first page of Membership Data table report.

2. Print the report.

 Click this button on the toolbar to print the report.

 Click to return to the Database window.

Reinforcing the Exercise

1. Errors in a table record can be corrected.

2. A number of field editing commands are available.

3. Press (SHIFT) + (F2) to issue the Zoom command and open the Zoom dialog box for entering text in a Memo field.

4. You can obtain a report of a table's contents quickly by clicking the Print button on the toolbar.

5. A report prints every field of each record in a grid format.

SESSION REVIEW

The term *database* is synonymous with *receptacle* for holding data tables, forms, queries, and so forth. A table consists of records that hold information about some type of business entity or transaction. Each record contains pieces of data, called fields, that relate to the transaction.

When designing the format of the table to hold data, you must keep future processing needs in mind. This may mean separating name fields into last name, first name, and middle initial fields so the computer can arrange the records in alphabetical order by last name.

Access 97 is a combination menu-driven and command-driven software package. It must be run from Windows on a hard disk drive.

Before creating an Access table, you must plan the field name, field length, and type of data to be used for each field and place this information in the structure of the table. The structure is built by clicking the New button on the Database window toolbar. Once you have defined the table structure, you can add records to the table or edit existing records by using the Datasheet window.

In the Datasheet window, field names appear at the top of the window, and the records and fields appear in a grid. You can use shortcut commands as well as cursor-movement keys to position the cursor and move from one record to the next within a table.

You use the Print button on the toolbar to quickly generate a printout, or report, of the table. If the records are long, the report will consist of several pages.

KEY TERMS AND CONCEPTS

AutoNumber field 6–10	key 6–2	relational database 6–2
Currency field 6–9	Memo field 6–9	report 6–24
database 6–2	menu-driven 6–3	secondary key 6–2
Database window 6–6	Number field 6–9	speedbar 6–15
Datasheet window 6–15	OLE object field 6–10	table 6–2
data type 6–9	primary key 6–2	table structure 6–2
Date/Time field 6–9	Program mode 6–3	Text field 6–9
field 6–2	record 6–2	Yes/No field 6–9
Field Properties box 6–10		

SESSION QUIZ

Multiple Choice

1. Which of the following terms is not related to a database application?
   a. table
   b. cell
   c. record
   d. field

2. Which of the following commands/features lets you place records in a database table?
   a. Catalog
   b. Datasheet window
   c. Append
   d. Add Records

3. Access buttons used to replace menu command sequences are found in the
   _____ .
   a. speedbar
   b. datasheet GOTO bar
   c. SpeedTool
   d. all of the above
   e. none of the above

4. Which of the following statements is true with respect to designing a table?
   a. Only one piece of data should be placed in a field.
   b. A table can hold information about two or more applications.
   c. A record holds one piece of data about an entity.
   d. None of the above.

5. Which of the following are valid data types for use with Access?
   a. Text
   b. Number
   c. Memo
   d. Date/Time
   e. Currency
   f. all of the above

True/False

6. The Access 97 package, as covered in this textbook, is strictly menu-driven.

7. Access 97 places all entities related to an application in a database.

8. When exiting Access, it is advisable to use the Close button or the File, Exit command sequence to avoid data loss or file corruption.

9. The Access package makes use of the arrow keys as well as other commands in the Datasheet window for cursor movement.

10. The datasheet speedbar buttons let you move forward and backward in a table.

SESSION REVIEW EXERCISES

1. Define or describe each of the following:
   a. database table
   b. menu-driven
   c. table structure

2. The entity used to hold tables, queries, reports, and so forth about a record-keeping application is called a _____ .

3. The Datasheet _____ contains buttons that you can click to move around in a table.

4. A _____ is a storage entity for a database. It is made up of records that contain data about a single thing.

5. Before you turn off the computer, you must properly exit to the _____ _____ to avoid possible data loss.

6. The _____ key is the unique identifier for a particular record.

7. A _____ contains all objects dealing with a set of related tables.

8. A field name can have up to _____ characters.

9. Use the _____ option of the context menu opened in the Database window to see a listing of the database name, description, last date modified, date created, type, and owner.

10. Open a table by double-clicking the table name in the _____ window.

11. The Datasheet window _____ at the bottom of the Datasheet window gives the physical location (record number) of a record in a table.

12. Click the _____ button on the Access title bar to exit Access and return to Windows.

13. The design of a table (field names and data type) is called the table _____ .

14. Use the _____ command from the context menu to change the name of an existing database table.

15. A phone number is typically defined as a _____ data type.

16. Access automatically places a _____ filename extension on a database file.

17. When you are editing the contents of a field, you can erase the field's contents by pressing the _____ key when the field is in reverse video.

18. A Memo field is placed in a file by pressing _____ + _____ , the Zoom command.

19. When defining a Text field, you typically want to change the Field Size entry in the _____ tab contained in the Field Properties box for that field.

20. When in the Datasheet window, you can move to the right one field or column at a time by pressing _____ or _____ .

COMPUTER EXERCISES

To do the following exercises, you must activate the Projects database using the Open an Existing Database option of the opening dialog box.

1. Create a table called Paymast. It should have the following structure:

Field	Field Name	Type	Width
1	EMPLOYEE ID	Text	4 Primary key
2	DEPARTMENT	Text	2
3	FIRST NAME	Text	10
4	INIT	Text	1
5	LAST NAME	Text	12
6	PAY RATE	Currency	Standard
7	YTD GROSS	Currency	Standard

2. Enter the following records in the Paymast table:

Record#	EMP. ID	DPT.	FIRST NAME	INIT.	LAST NAME	PAY RATE	YTD GROSS
1	1232	10	Arthur	D	Winnakor	10.50	12560.00
2	9234	15	Mildred	T	Klassen	12.75	15960.00
3	4873	10	Martin	D	Wilhelm	8.75	9450.00
4	2956	15	Monica	D	Wilson	9.50	7694.00
5	9643	10	Stephanie	D	Grapchek	7.75	8964.00

3. Add the following records to the Paymast table:

Record#	EMP. ID	DPT.	FIRST NAME	INIT.	LAST NAME	PAY RATE	YTD GROSS
6	7650	10	Willard	D	Farnsworth	8.75	1200.00
7	7645	10	Margery	T	Fitzgibbons	9.75	3570.00
8	6594	15	Tomas	D	Ruiz	7.75	2975.00
9	9346	20	Alan	D	Chapin	9.50	6750.00
10	6295	20	Alfred	D	Benjamin	5.75	2375.00
11	3957	20	William	D	Rich	8.50	3460.00
12	4075	15					

4. Correct any errors in Paymast. Also use the Datasheet window to place your name in the name fields for record 12.

5. Print the Paymast table.

INTERNET EXERCISES

1. Get additional information about Access.
   a. Access Microsoft's home page with your browser (http://www.microsoft.com).
   b. Click the Products button at the top of the Web page. Once that page is displayed, choose Access 97 for Windows 95 from the list of products.
   c. Click the Visit the Microsoft® Access 97 for Windows® 95 Website link located in the Contents bar on the left side of the screen.
   d. Print the first page of this Web site.

SESSION 2

Manipulating and Sorting Tables

After completing this session, you should be able to:

➤ Use the Datasheet window

➤ Enter commands using the Access menu structure

➤ Use a number of table-manipulation commands

➤ Find records in a table

➤ Sort records in a table

➤ Use a filter to sort a table

➤ Use a filter to select specific records

 Isabel and Alice now want to explore a number of ways in which they can manipulate the data they have entered in a table. Isabel wants to show Alice various ways to display records that are stored in a table and to display information to the screen.

Alice wants to know how to locate records that have a specific field content as well as how to sort records. She is interested in single-field and multiple-field sorts.

This session reinforces the use of the Datasheet window and a number of table-manipulation commands. It also shows how to sort tables and locate records in a table by using commands issued via the Access menus.

WORKING IN THE DATASHEET WINDOW

As you discovered in Session 1, the Datasheet window is Access's main method of displaying the records of an open (active) table. You can use this window to make changes to a table. The results of many Access commands appear in the Datasheet window. It is therefore important that you understand how various commands work within this window.

The usual method of opening this window is by double-clicking the desired table in the list displayed in the Database window. You will need to maximize the Datasheet window to work in it easily. Figure 2.1 shows the Membership Data table displayed in a maximized Datasheet window.

MEMBERSHIP	SALUTATION	FIRST NAME	MIDDLE INITIA	LAST NAME	ADDRESS	C
17634	Ms.	Denise	J	Witherspoon	23 Payne Place	Norma
27245	Mr.	Arthur	K	Adams	927 Anchor	Leroy
27823	Mrs.	John	C	Pope	123 Hackberry	Bloom
36784	Mr.	Randal	C	Hart	344 W. Chestnu	Bloom
38724	Ms.	Jeanette	O	Alazar	1421 Haywood	Norma
40267	Mr.	Gerald	I	McDermott	1225 W. Market	Bloom
40275	Ms.	Donna	L	Barnes	127 E. Market	Bloom
41833	Mr.	Alfred	M	Kuper	202 N. Prospec	Bloom
58404	Dr.	John	J	Puckett	3542 Woodbine	Bloom
63198	Dr.	Federico	J	Gonzalez	1425 W. Colleg	Norma
67392	Ms	Joanne	T	Arnold	814 W. Jacksor	Leroy
75097	Dr.	Alberta	D	Crandall	1232 W. Longw	Bloom
89301	Ms.	Juanita	Q	Romero	1018 W. Prairie	Norma
94219	Mrs.	Kim	F	Schulz	123 W.Willow	Norma
95388	Mr.	Andy	L	Nowlin	401 S. Clay	Leroy

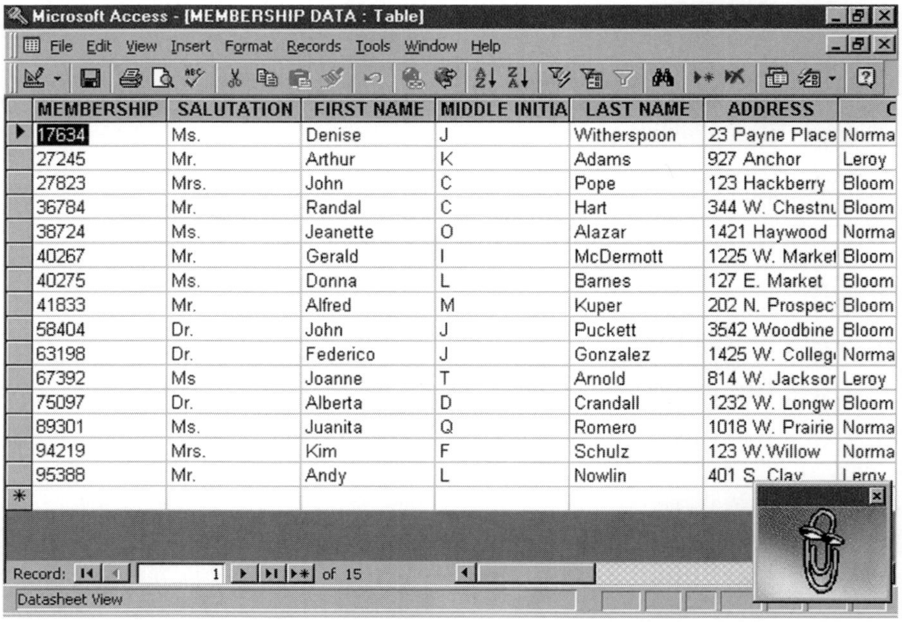

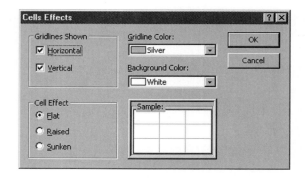

Figure 2.1
The open Membership Data table displayed in the maximized Datasheet window.

Deleting and Restoring Gridlines

Access automatically includes **gridlines** around each cell of the table displayed in the Datasheet window. For most people, these gridlines increase the readability of the table by helping the eye track along the appropriate line (record). For others, however, these gridlines can be distracting. If you want to get rid of the gridlines, issue the Format, Cells command sequence. The Cells Effects dialog box opens as shown in Figure 2.2.

If you click the Horizontal and Vertical options to get rid of the check marks (which appear by default), the gridlines will disappear (Figure 2.3). If you then issue the Print command to print the table, the printed table along with column headings will be the only portions of the report to be included within printed lines. To restore the gridlines, you reissue

Figure 2.2
The Cells Effects dialog box controls how the datasheet cells will appear on screen.

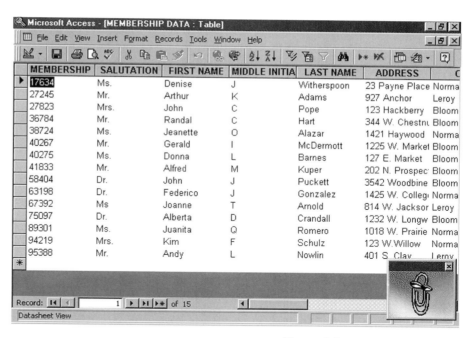

Figure 2.3
The Membership Data table without gridlines.

the Format, Cells command sequence and click Horizontal and Vertical in the Cells Effects dialog box.

Changing the Display Width of a Field   F̲ormat, C̲olumn Width . . .

When working on the Datasheet window, you may want to resize one or more columns so additional fields can appear onscreen. Do this either by using the mouse to drag a column's border to the desired location or by selecting the entire column and entering a new column width in the Column Width dialog box. When you resize a column or field onscreen, only the display is altered. The table remains unchanged. The field that is resized is the field at the cursor location.

(The preceeding discussion makes use of the mouse to resize a column in one of two ways: by dragging or by selecting.)

Dragging

You can change the width of a column by placing the cursor on the border of the cell that contains the field name (in the table heading). The cursor changes into a bar with right and left arrows (↔). You then drag the cell border to the right to increase column width or to the left to decrease column width.

Pointing

You can use the pointing method by placing the pointer anywhere in the cell that contains the field name. The pointer turns into a large down arrow (↓). When you click the mouse, the entire column is selected and is

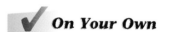

On Your Own

Examine how the various options in the Cells Effects dialog box affect the appearance of the Datasheet window. When you have finished experimenting, return the Datasheet window to its original appearance using the settings shown in Figure 2.1.

Figure 2.4
The Middle Initial column selected.

displayed in reverse video (Figure 2.4). You can then issue the Format, Column Width command sequence. The Column Width dialog box opens (Figure 2.5). You can enter the new column width in the text box, or you can click the Best Fit button to allow Access to reset the width. (You are better off trying to reset it yourself because Access doesn't do a very good job of guessing.) Figure 2.6 shows the column width set to 2.

You can also select multiple columns at one time and reset their widths all at once. To select multiple columns, you can either hold down (SHIFT) and click the beginning and ending columns, or drag the pointer

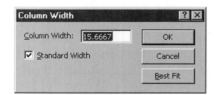

Figure 2.5
The Column Width dialog box.

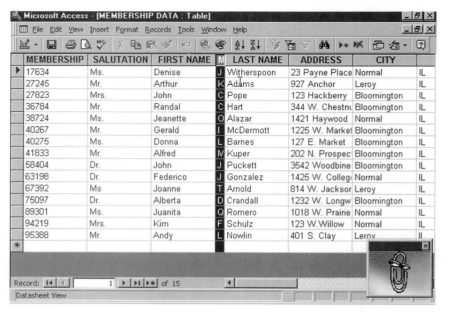

Figure 2.6
The Middle Initial column width set to 2.

Figure 2.7
The Salutation through Address fields selected.

across the field names at the top of the Datasheet window. Figure 2.7 shows the Salutation through Address columns selected.

If you try to close the Datasheet window to return to the Database window, Access does not automatically save changes that you have made to the appearance of the table as it does when you change the contents of a record. When you click the Close button of the Datasheet window, Access displays the dialog box shown in Figure 2.8, asking you whether you want to save the changes to the table in the database. Many times you just want to make temporary changes to the table for use in the Datasheet window and, therefore, do not want to save those changes to the table itself.

Figure 2.8
The dialog box prompting you about saving changes to the database table.

Hands-On Exercise: Resizing Fields

Alice wants to resize some of the fields in the Membership Data table.

1. **Start Access and open the Membership database.**

2. **Open the Membership Data table.**

Membership Data Double-click the Membership Data table in the Database window. Maximize the datasheet window.

3. **Resize the Address field by using the Column Width dialog box.**

ADDRESS Position the pointer in the cell that contains the Address field name. Wait for the pointer to become a large down arrow.

Click Click to select the Address column (Figure 2.9).

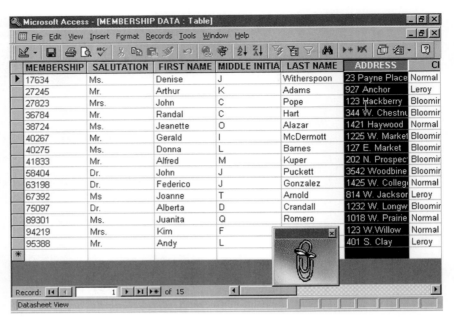

Figure 2.9
The datasheet with the Address field selected.

Format	Click to open the Format menu.
Column Width . . .	Click to open the Column Width dialog box (Figure 2.10).

Type the new column width: **21**

(ENTER)	Press to finalize the change.
Click	Click anywhere to turn off the selection.

4. **Repeat step 3 to resize the Middle Initial field to 2.** The screen should look like Figure 2.11.

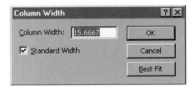

Figure 2.10
The Column Width dialog box.

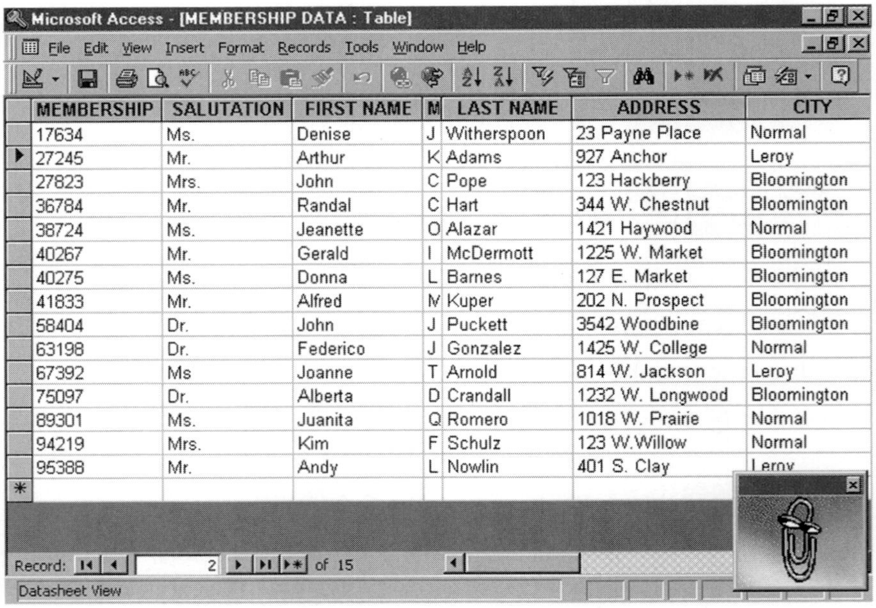

Figure 2.11
The resized Address field.

5. **Resize the Salutation field by dragging.**

	Position the pointer on the right border of the cell that contains the Salutation field name. The pointer changes to a bar with right and left arrows.
Drag	Drag the pointer until the field is just wide enough to fit the largest entry.

6. **Repeat step 5 to resize the following fields by dragging.** Use Figure 2.12 as a guide.

   First Name

   Last Name

   City

   State

   Zip

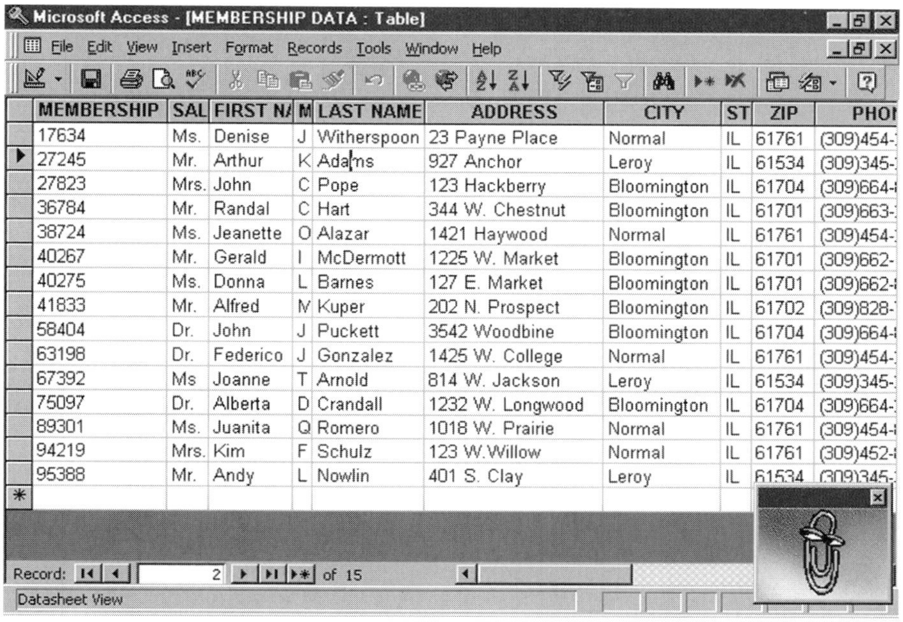

Microsoft Access - [MEMBERSHIP DATA : Table]

	MEMBERSHIP	SAL	FIRST N/	M	LAST NAME	ADDRESS	CITY	ST	ZIP	PHOI
	17634	Ms.	Denise	J	Witherspoon	23 Payne Place	Normal	IL	61761	(309)454-
▶	27245	Mr.	Arthur	K	Adams	927 Anchor	Leroy	IL	61534	(309)345-
	27823	Mrs.	John	C	Pope	123 Hackberry	Bloomington	IL	61704	(309)664-
	36784	Mr.	Randal	C	Hart	344 W. Chestnut	Bloomington	IL	61701	(309)663-
	38724	Ms.	Jeanette	O	Alazar	1421 Haywood	Normal	IL	61761	(309)454-
	40267	Mr.	Gerald	I	McDermott	1225 W. Market	Bloomington	IL	61701	(309)662-
	40275	Ms.	Donna	L	Barnes	127 E. Market	Bloomington	IL	61701	(309)662-
	41833	Mr.	Alfred	M	Kuper	202 N. Prospect	Bloomington	IL	61702	(309)828-
	58404	Dr.	John	J	Puckett	3542 Woodbine	Bloomington	IL	61704	(309)664-
	63198	Dr.	Federico	J	Gonzalez	1425 W. College	Normal	IL	61761	(309)454-
	67392	Ms	Joanne	T	Arnold	814 W. Jackson	Leroy	IL	61534	(309)345-
	75097	Dr.	Alberta	D	Crandall	1232 W. Longwood	Bloomington	IL	61704	(309)664-
	89301	Ms.	Juanita	Q	Romero	1018 W. Prairie	Normal	IL	61761	(309)454-
	94219	Mrs.	Kim	F	Schulz	123 W.Willow	Normal	IL	61761	(309)452-
	95388	Mr.	Andy	L	Nowlin	401 S. Clay	Leroy	IL	61534	(309)345-
*										

Record: 2 of 15

Datasheet View

Figure 2.12
The other fields resized by dragging.

Reinforcing the Exercise

1. You can resize a column by using a drag operation initiated at the cell that contains the field name.
2. You can also resize a column by selecting the column, issuing the Format, Column Width command sequence, and then entering the desired width in the Column Width dialog box.

Moving a Field

Access 97 allows you to move entire fields (columns) from one location in the table to another. First you select the column. Then you position the pointer in the selected column's field name and press and hold the left mouse button. A square should appear beneath the pointer. Drag the pointer to the desired location. A thin black line appears between the columns as you drag the field to the desired location. Once the field is in the appropriate location, you can release the mouse button.

Hands-On Exercise: Moving a Field

MIDDLE INITIAL	Position the pointer in the Middle Initial field name. The pointer turns into a large down arrow.
Click	Click on the field name to select the column.
Click and hold	Position the pointer in the Middle Initial field name again and click. A square appears below the pointer arrow, indicating that you can move this column.
Drag	Drag the Middle Initial field to the right until a dark line appears between the Last Name and address fields.
Release	Release the mouse button. The table should look like Figure 2.13.

Hiding a Field   **F**ormat, **H**ide Columns

Access also allows you to hide fields so that you can group desired fields on one screen to make the table more readable. This is accomplished by selecting a column or columns and then issuing the Format, Hide Columns command sequence. The fields can later be restored using the Format, Unhide Columns command sequence. You can also use a context menu to hide fields.

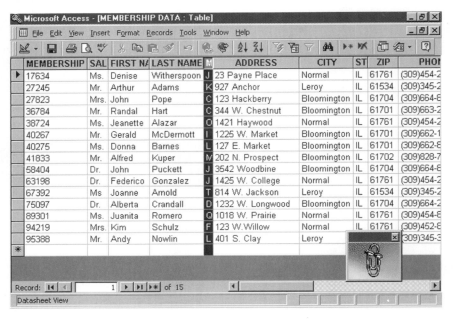

Figure 2.13
The Datasheet window with the Middle Initial field moved to a new location.

Hands-On Exercise: Hiding Fields

Alice wants to hide the Salutation and Middle Initial fields so that identifying information about a member is available on one screen.

1.   **Hide the salutation field.**

SALUTATION	Position the pointer in the Salutation field name, and wait for the pointer to become a large down arrow.
Click	Click on the field name to select the column.
Format	Click to open the Format menu.
Hide Columns	Click to hide the Salutation column. The Datasheet window should look like Figure 2.14.

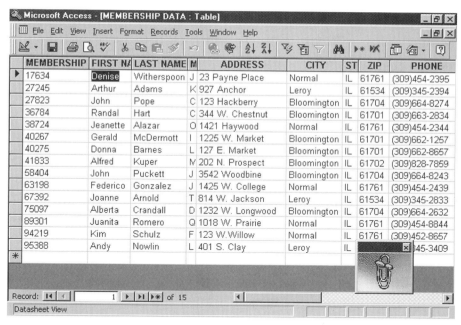

2. Hide the Middle Initial Field.

MIDDLE INITIAL Position the pointer in the Middle Initial field name, and wait for the pointer to become a large down arrow.

Click Click on the field name to select the column.

Format Open the Format menu.

Hide Columns Click to hide the Middle Initial column. Your Datasheet window should look like Figure 2.15.

Figure 2.14
The datasheet with the Saluta-tion field hidden.

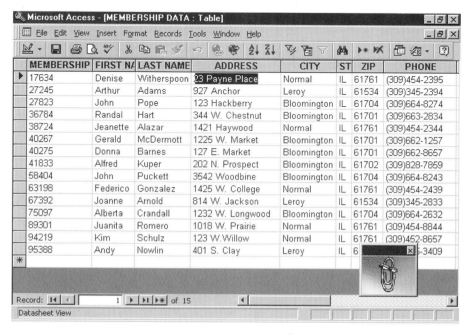

Figure 2.15
The datasheet with the Middle Initial field hidden.

3. **Restore the columns to the Datasheet window.**

Format   Click to open the Format menu.

Unhide Columns   Click to open the Unhide Columns dialog box (Figure 2.16). Fields that are included in the current datasheet are marked with a check.

MIDDLE INITIAL   Click to place this field back into the table.

SALUTATION   Click to place this field back into the table.

[Close]   Click to close the dialog box and return to the Datasheet window. The fields have been added to the datasheet.

Locking a Field Format, Freeze Columns

One problem with displaying records is that sometimes some of the identifying data is shifted off the screen when you view other parts of a record. If you want to make certain that some identifying fields of each record always appear on the screen, you issue the Format, Freeze Columns command sequence.

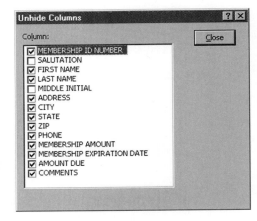

Figure 2.16
The Unhide Columns dialog box shows which fields are currently displayed in the Datasheet window.

Hands-On Exercise: Locking Fields

1. **Hide the Salutation field.**

SALUTATION   Position the pointer in the Salutation field name, and wait for the pointer to become a large down arrow.

Right-click   Right-click to select the column and open the context menu (Figure 2.17).

Hide Columns   Click to hide the Salutation column.

2. **Hide the Middle Initial column.**

MIDDLE INITIAL   Position the pointer in the Middle Initial field name, and wait for the pointer to become a large down arrow.

Right-click   Right-click to select the column and open the column context menu (Figure 2.17).

Hide Columns   Click to hide the Middle Initial column.

3. **Lock the Membership Number ID, First Name, and Last Name fields.**

MEMBERSHIP ID   Position the pointer in the Membership ID Number
NUMBER   field name, and wait for the pointer to become a large down arrow.

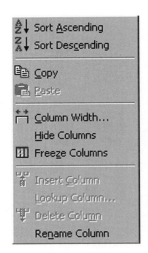

Figure 2.17
The column context menu.

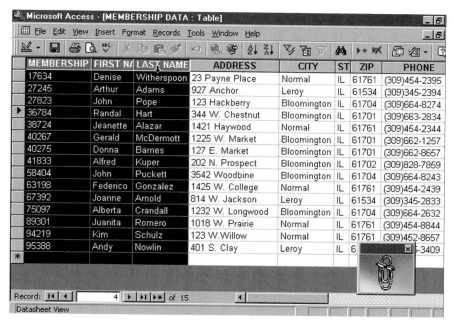

Figure 2.18
The first three columns of the datasheet are selected.

Click and drag	Click the mouse and drag to the Last Name field. All three columns should be selected (Figure 2.18). Continue to hold down the left button.
Right-click	While holding down the left mouse button, right-click to open the context menu.
Freeze Columns	Click to freeze the first three columns.
Click	Click anywhere to turn off the selection. A dark line now appears to the right of the frozen columns (Figure 2.19).

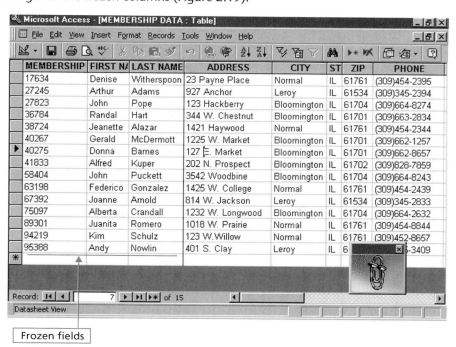

Frozen fields

Figure 2.19
A dark line now appears to the right of the frozen columns.

Click the right arrow of the horizontal scroll bar at the bottom of the Datasheet window to display the Amount Due field. You can see that the frozen fields remain as you move to the right (Figure 2.20).

MEMBERSHIP	FIRST NA	LAST NAME	MEMBERSHIP	AMOUNT DUE	COMMENTS
17634	Denise	Witherspoon	23-Oct-97	$150.00	
27245	Arthur	Adams	15-Aug-98	$253.00	
27823	John	Pope	23-Oct-99	$400.00	
36784	Randal	Hart	13-Dec-97	$150.00	
38724	Jeanette	Alazar	31-Mar-97	$35.00	
40267	Gerald	McDermott	12-Dec-97	$250.00	
40275	Donna	Barnes	23-Oct-99	$195.00	
41833	Alfred	Kuper	15-May-98	$25.00	
58404	John	Puckett	06-Jun-96	$80.00	
63198	Federico	Gonzalez	30-Nov-97	$500.00	
67392	Joanne	Arnold	31-Dec-98	$275.00	Joanne has sev
75097	Alberta	Crandall	23-Oct-98	$750.00	
89301	Juanita	Romero	20-Mar-98	$175.00	
94219	Kim	Schulz	30-Jun-97	$75.00	
95388	Andy	Nowlin	31-Jul-99	$0.00	
*				$0.00	

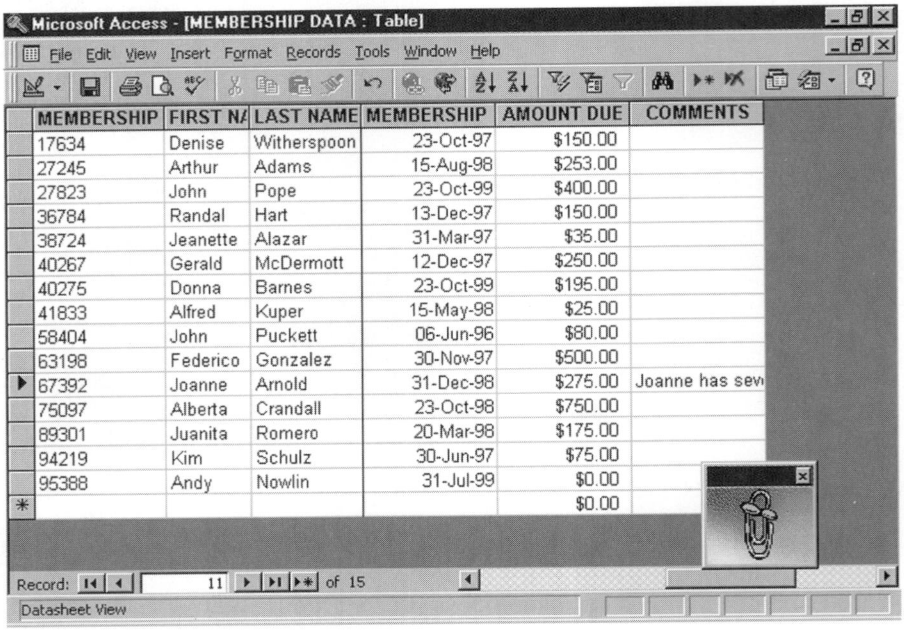

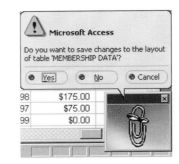

Figure 2.20
As you move to the right through the columns in the Datasheet window, the frozen columns remain where they are.

4. **Close the Membership Data table.**

Click to return the Datasheet window to its smaller size.

Click to close the Datasheet window. The Office Assistant asks what you want to do with the changes (Figure 2.21).

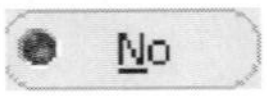

Click to close the Datasheet window without saving the changes.

Figure 2.21
The dialog box prompting you about the changes to the datasheet.

Reinforcing the Exercise

1. You can move fields to another location in the Datasheet window by using a drag operation.
2. If you don't want one or more columns to appear in the Datasheet window, you can hide them.
3. Fields with identifying information can be frozen on the screen so they are always displayed.

NAVIGATING THROUGH AND LOCATING RECORDS

This section introduces a number of ways to move the pointer to desired locations within a table. In addition, this section covers how to locate records in a table.

Using the Record Pointer

In the left margin of the Datasheet window, a right arrow called the **record pointer** helps you keep track of where you are within a table (Figure 2.22). The record number that appears in the speedbar when you are working in the Datasheet window is the current location of the record pointer.

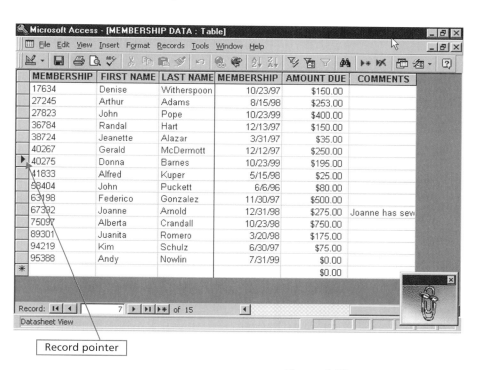

Record pointer

Figure 2.22
The record pointer marks the active record in the Datasheet window.

To move the record pointer from one location (record) in a table to another, you can use the arrow keys: Press the up arrow key to move to records located before the current one, and press the down arrow key to advance to records below the current one.

Using arrow keys to position the record pointer is adequate when your tables contain only a few records. If you have several thousand records, however, it would take far too long. A faster way to move the record pointer within a large table is to use the scroll bar in a drag operation. As you drag the scroll box down the vertical scroll bar, a box displays the record pointer location (Figure 2.23). You can also use the speedbar to move around in a table quickly. Also, you can double-click the record number displayed in the speedbar, type the number of the record you want to go to, and then press (ENTER).

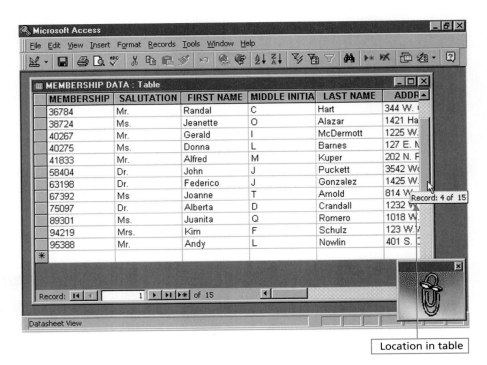

Location in table

Figure 2.23
The location box appears over
the scroll box when you are issuing a drag operation.

Hands-On Exercise: Record Pointer Manipulation

1. **Activate the Membership database if necessary.**

2. **Open the Membership Data table.**

**MEMBERSHIP
DATA**   Double-click the Membership Data table in the Database
                     window. The Datasheet window should resemble Figure
                     2.24. Notice that the speedbar shows that the current po-
                     sition of the record pointer is record 1 of 15.

3. **Move ahead to another record in the table.**

⊥   Press the down arrow three times. Notice that the Record
                     speedbar shows you are at record 4 of 15.

4. **Move among the records by using the speedbar at the bottom of the
   Datasheet window.**

                  Click to move to the last record. Notice that the record
                     number displayed is 15 of 15.

                  Click to move to the first record. Notice that the record
                     number displayed is 1 of 15.

                  Click three times to move the record pointer to record 4.

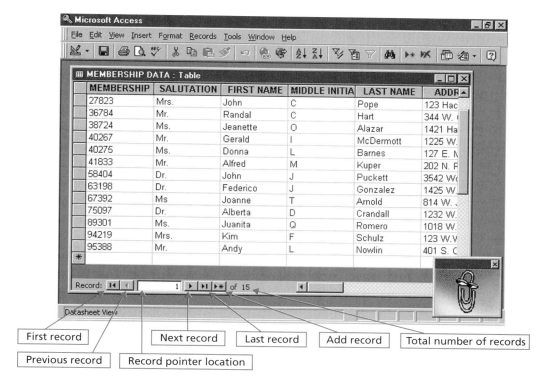

Double-click

Double-click the record number in the speedbar.

Type: **12**

(ENTER)

Press to move to record 12.

Figure 2.24
The Record entry of the speed-bar shows the pointer location in the table.

Reinforcing the Exercise

1. The record pointer is the Access term for the cursor.
2. The speedbar displays the location of the record pointer and the total number of records, and contains navigation buttons and a scroll bar.
3. The speedbar buttons allow you to move from record to record within the table.
4. To move quickly among records, you can use the Datasheet window's vertical scroll bar, or you can double-click the record number displayed in the speedbar, enter the number of the record you desire, and then press (ENTER).

Locating Records Using Find   **Edit, Find or** 🔍

Moving to a particular record using the techniques described in the previous section is a straightforward task as long as you know the record number. What happens, however, when you do not know the record number? For such situations, Access provides the Find dialog box, in which you specify the field to be searched as well as the characters to search for. Access then compares those with the contents of the specified field for each record. The search starts with the first record or the current record and ends with the last record.

You can click the Find button on the toolbar to open the Find dialog box to specify criteria for locating records in a table. The title bar of the dialog box indicates that the record pointer was positioned in the Last Name field when the Find command was issued (Figure 2.25). Enter the text you want to search for in the Find What text box. The field to be searched defaults to the field in which the record pointer resides. The following options in the dialog box can also be used to control the search:

TIMELY TIP

You can also open the Find dialog box by any of the following methods:

- Using the shortcut command (CTRL) + **F**.
- Issuing the command sequence Edit, Find.

Figure 2.25
The Find dialog box.

- The Search list box controls the direction in which the search is to take place: Forward (down), Backward (up), or All (from the beginning).

- The Match list box indicates how the match is to occur: Whole Field, Any Part of Field, or Start of Field.

- The Match Case check box finds records that match the case of the search text exactly. If, for example, you choose this option and specify *Access* as your search text, the program will ignore records that contain the word *access* or *ACCESS*.

- The Search Fields as Formatted option finds data based on its display format. Searches using this method are usually slower than a text-based search.

- The Search Only Current Field option includes only the current column in the search.

- The Find First command button finds the first occurrence of the search string.

- The Find Next button finds subsequent occurrences of the search string.

- The Close button allows you to return to the Datasheet window and view the located record.

When specifying search criteria, you can use the two wildcard characters * and ?. The ? represents one character, and the * specifies any remaining characters. For example, the search criteria *fo?* would find *fog* and *for*, and the search criteria *fo** would find *fog, for, foot, form, football,* and so on.

TIMELY TIP

To find subsequent occurrences, you can use the shortcut command (CTRL) + **F** or click the Find toolbar button and then click the Find Next Command button.

Hands-On Exercise: Locating Records

Alice needs to find the record with a First Name field that has the contents *Kim*.

1. **Open the Membership Data table.** Click the First Name field of the first record.

2. **Find the record with the First Name field contents of** *Kim.*

    Click this toolbar button to open the Find dialog box (Figure 2.26).

Type the search criteria in the Find What text box: **Kim**

Retain the All and the Current Field defaults.

Find First Click this command button to find the first record with the match. Notice that the record number in the speedbar is 14 of 15, indicating that a match has been found in record 14.

Figure 2.26
The Find dialog box.

Close Click to view the record that has generated the match (Figure 2.27).

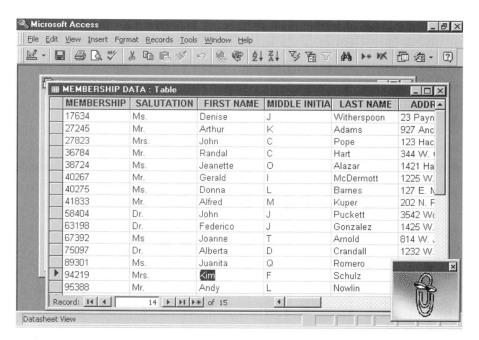

Figure 2.27
Record 14 contains a match of *Kim* in the First Name field.

3. **Start another search.**

CITY Click the City field name.

 Click to open the Find dialog box.

4. **Find any record that has *Bloomington* in the city field.**

Type the search criterion in the Find What text box: **Blo***

Find First	Click to find the first occurrence. You should get a match on record 3 of 15.
Find Next	Click to find the next occurrence. You should get a match on record 4 of 15.
Find Next	Click to find the next occurrence. You should get a match on record 6 of 15.
Close	Click to terminate the search and return to the Datasheet window.
	Click this button in the Datasheet window to close the Membership Data table.

In a successful search, the record number that matches the search criterion appears at the bottom of the Access window. If the search fails, an alert dialog box (Figure 2.28) indicates that the value was not found.

Reinforcing the Exercise

1. The Find dialog box allows you to indicate the field contents that you are looking for.
2. One way to open the Find dialog box is to click the Find button on the toolbar.
3. The search starts with either the current record or the first record and ends with the last record.
4. You can use wildcard characters (* and ?) to locate data in a Find operation.

SORTING RECORDS

The Sort command physically rearranges records according to values contained in one or more specific fields of each record. To sort on one field, you click anywhere within that field and then click either the Sort Ascending or the Sort Descending button on the toolbar. To sort on multiple fields, you use the Records, Filter, Advanced Filter/Sort command sequence.

Sorting on One Field

Before sorting a table on one field, you must designate the key field for sorting by placing the record pointer in that field and clicking or by selecting the entire column. Then you click the Sort Ascending or Sort Descending button of the toolbar. The changes made by the Sort command do not affect the original table unless you issue a Save command. The unsorted Membership Data table and the sort buttons are shown in Figure 2.29.

Figure 2.28
The alert dialog box that appears when no record meets the criteria or when the end of the table has been reached (after the last match).

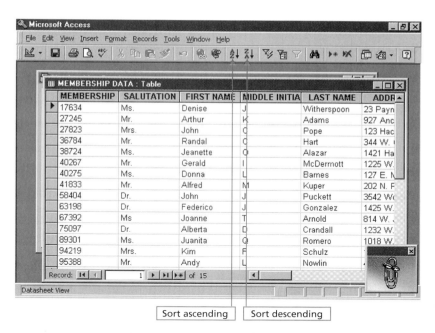

Sort ascending   Sort descending

Figure 2.29
The unsorted Membership Data table.

Hands-On Exercise: Sorting by Last Name

1. If necessary, activate the Membership database.

2. Open the Membership Data table.

3. Sort by last name in ascending order.

Click		Click the Last Name field of any record in the table.

 Click to begin the sort operation. The Membership Data table is now sorted in ascending order by the last names (Figure 2.30).

4. Sort the table in order by zip code.

5. Sort the table in order by city.

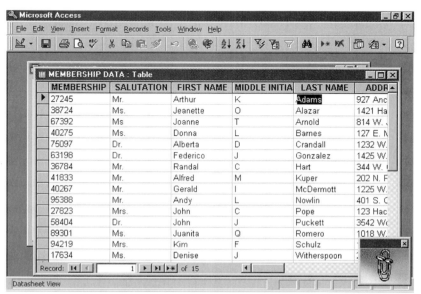

Figure 2.30
The Membership Data table sorted in ascending order by last name.

Reinforcing the Exercise

1. You use the Sort command to rearrange records according to values contained in one or more fields that you specify.

2. To sort by one field, you first select the field and then click either the Sort Ascending or the Sort Descending button on the toolbar.

3. The changes made by the Sort command do not change the table permanently unless you issue a Save command.

Sorting by Multiple Fields   Records, Filter, Advanced Filter/Sort . . .

When Access performs a sort, it uses what it calls a **filter** to process the data and rearrange it in the table based on the selected column. With a one-field sort, Access automatically applies the selected field to the filter. However, with a multiple-field sort, you must specify the fields to be included in the filter process.

To specify a multiple-field sort, you issue the Records, Filter, Advanced Filter/Sort command sequence. The Filter dialog box appears as shown in Figure 2.31. The bottom portion of the Filter dialog box allows you to specify the fields to be included in the sort process. The first field is assumed to be the field containing the mouse pointer. You then execute the sort by clicking the Apply Filter/Sort button on the toolbar.

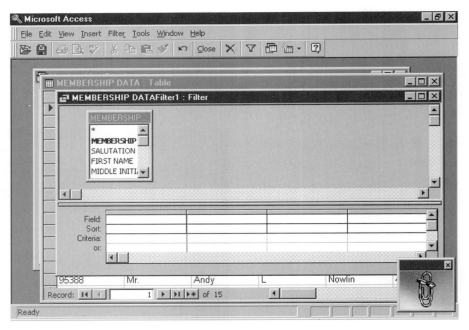

Figure 2.31
The Filter dialog box used for defining multiple-field sorts.

Hands-On Exercise: Sorting by Name Within City

1. If necessary, activate the Membership Data table of the Membership database.

2. Build the sort filter.

Records Click to open the Records menu.

Filter Click to open the Filter menu.

Advanced Filter/ Sort . . . Click to open the Filter dialog box shown in Figure 2.32. If CITY does not appear in the Field portion of the Filter dialog box, click the down arrow to the right of the field box and then select the City field. Also select Ascending in the Sort field if necessary.

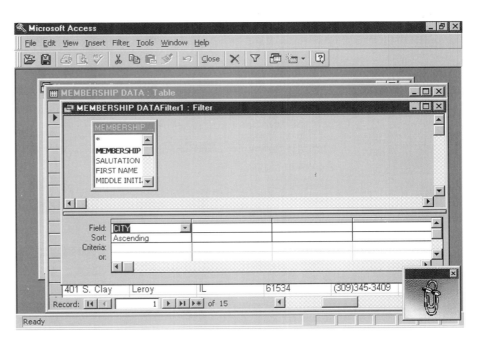

Figure 2.32
The Filter dialog box with the City field already entered as the first sort field.

3. Define the second sort field.

Click Click the second column of the Field box.

 Click the down arrow in the Field box. A list box like that depicted in Figure 2.33 appears.

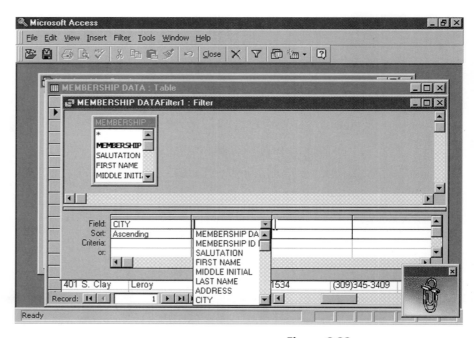

Figure 2.33
The list box for determining the next sort field.

LAST NAME	Click to include this field in the sort.
Click	Click the Sort cell beneath the Last Name entry to activate the Sort box for that field.
	Click the down arrow of the Sort box to see the list box shown in Figure 2.34.

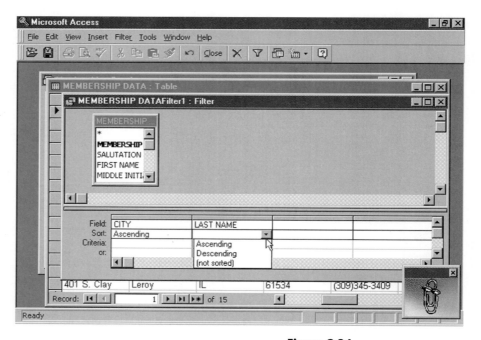

Figure 2.34
The list box for selecting the order in which a column is to be sorted.

Ascending   Click to select ascending order. If you fail to make a selection, Access defaults to (not sorted).

Your completed Filter dialog box should look like Figure 2.35.

4. **Perform the sort.**

Click the Apply Filter/Sort button on the toolbar (Figure 2.35) to perform the sort and return to the Datasheet window. Your screen should look like Figure 2.36. (You may have to use the scroll arrows to get to the beginning of the table.)

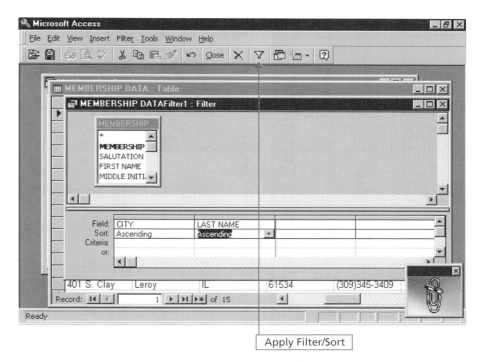

Figure 2.35
The completed Filter dialog box for the sort.

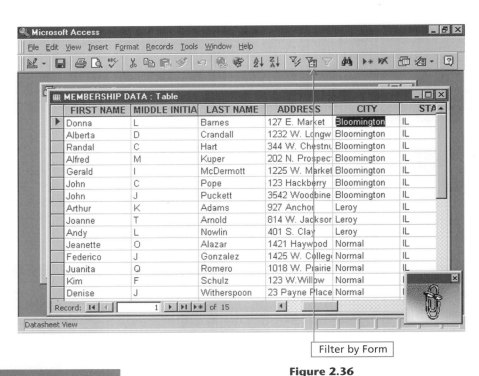

Filter by Form

Figure 2.36
The Membership Data table sorted in order by name within city.

Reinforcing the Exercise

1. To sort by more than one field, you use the Filter dialog box.

2. You open the Filter dialog box by issuing the Records, Filter, Advanced Filter/Sort command sequence.

3. After you complete the Filter dialog box, you execute the sort by clicking the Apply Filter/Sort button on the toolbar.

Displaying Selected Records

You can also use the Access filter to display only those records that meet certain criteria. If you have an extremely large table, you may not want to include all records in an operation. To display only certain records, you click the Filter by Form button on the toolbar (Figure 2.36) and use the Filter by Form Window shown in Figure 2.37.

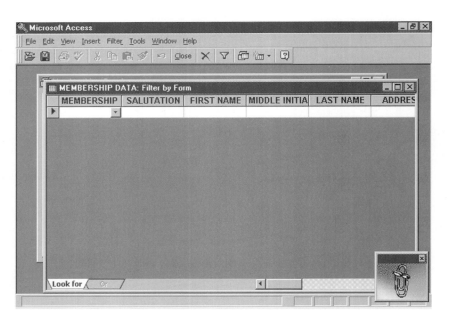

Figure 2.37
The Filter by Form window opens when you click the Filter by Form button on the toolbar.

Hands-On Exercise: Creating a Filter to Display Only Certain Records

Alice wants to create a form of the Membership Data table that includes only those records with 61761 in the Zip field.

1. **If necessary, activate the Membership Data table of the Membership database.**

2. **Build the sort filter.**

   Click this toolbar button to open the Filter by Form window shown in Figure 2.38. Notice that this form has all of the field names and an empty row for entering selection criteria.

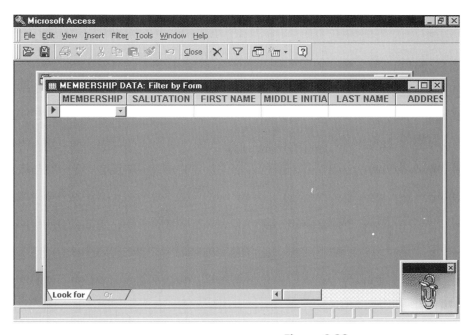

Figure 2.38
The Filter by Form window.

3. **Define the selection field.**

   Click the right scroll arrow of the speedbar until you see the Zip field.

Click   Click the blank cell beneath the Zip field name.

4. **Enter the selection criteria.**

Enter the selection criteria: **61761**

Since the desired zip code is in a text cell, Access automatically places the text between double quotation marks. The Filter by Form window should look like Figure 2.39.

TIMELY TIP

You can also click the down arrow button in the cell to display the various values contained in the Zip field and then select one to establish filter criteria.

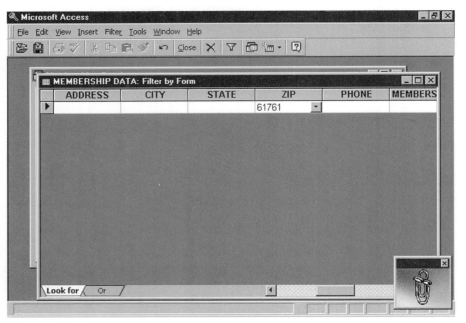

Figure 2.39
The completed Filter by Form window for getting only those records with a zip code of 61761.

5. **Perform the selection.**

 Click the Apply Filter button on the toolbar to perform the selection and return to the Datasheet window. The screen should look like Figure 2.40.

(You may have to move the screen to the right using the scroll arrows.)

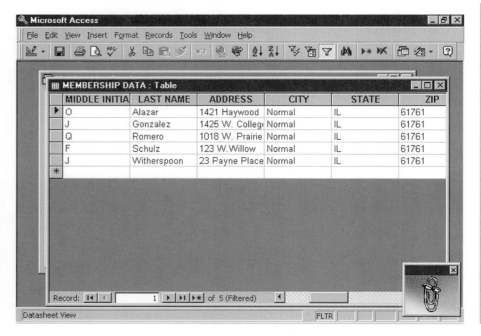

Figure 2.40
The records that match the filter criteria.

6. Close the Datasheet window.

     Click to close the Datasheet window. Access now prompts
you about saving design information.

     Click to return to the Database window without saving
anything.

Reinforcing the Exercise

1. To display only selected fields in a table, you use the Filter by Form window.
2. You click the Filter By Form toolbar button to open the Filter by Form window.
3. In the proper field location of the Filter by Form window, specify the desired field contents of records to be included in the selection.

SESSION REVIEW

The Datasheet window is Access's tool for displaying database tables. You can use the Datasheet window to change column widths, lock fields so they are always displayed, and move fields. From the Datasheet window, you can quickly move through a table and manually make changes to selected records.

   The speedbar at the bottom of the Datasheet window provides a number of ways to position the record pointer. The Find dialog box lets you search table fields for specific values.

   Access provides the Sort command to order records within a table. The Sort command creates tables in which the records are sorted by one or more specified fields.

   You use the Filter dialog box to sort selected records from a table. It must be used for multiple-field sorts. You use the Filter by Form window to enter field criteria for selecting records to be displayed in the Datasheet window.

KEY TERMS AND CONCEPTS

filter 6–50   gridlines 6-32   record pointer 6-43

SESSION QUIZ

Multiple Choice

1. Which of the following statements about sorting is/are false?
   a. It makes use of an Access filter.
   b. A single-field sort involves only clicking an icon after selecting a field.
   c. A multiple-key sort is impossible.
   d. You are allowed to sort on only one field at a time.

2. Which of the following statements about the record pointer is/are true?
   a. The record pointer always indicates which record is currently ready to have some task performed against it.
   b. The record pointer location can always be seen in the toolbar.
   c. The record pointer location can always be seen in the speedbar.
   d. All of the above statements are false.

3. Which command finds records in a table?
   a. Find
   b. Browse
   c. List
   d. Index
   e. Continue

4. Which of the following tasks is/are not permitted in the Datasheet window?
   a. changing column width
   b. hiding a column
   c. moving a column
   d. All of the above are permitted.

5. Which speedbar button moves the record pointer to the last record in a table?
   a.
   b.
   c.
   d.

True/False

6. A table field in the Datasheet window can only be resized using a drag operation.

7. Access allows you to move a field in the Datasheet window by dragging it to a new location.

8. To make certain that a field always appears, use the Lock Fields command.

9. You use the Filter dialog box for specifying a multiple key sort.

10. The speedbar allows you to move from record to record in a table.

SESSION REVIEW EXERCISES

1. Define or describe each of the following:
   a. filter
   b. Find command

2. The _____ window is used to display the records in a table.

3. To open the datasheet window, _____ the desired table listed in the Database window.

4. Use the _____ _____ dialog box to control the appearance of gridlines on the datasheet.

5. Using the mouse in a _____ operation allows you to resize a table field in the datasheet.

6. Use the _____ _____ dialog box to change the width of a field in the Datasheet window.

7. Moving a column involves first selecting the column and then using a _____ operation to move it to another location.

8. Use the _____ _____ command to inhibit the display of a table column.

9. The _____ _____ dialog box allows you to redisplay a hidden table column.

10. Use the Format, _____ _____ command sequence to lock the display of a column in the Datasheet window.

11. The record _____ always tells you where you are in a table.

12. The _____ has buttons that allow you to move from one record to another in a table.

13. The _____ speedbar button sends you to the beginning of the last record in a table.

14. Use the _____ dialog box to locate records with specific values in a table.

15. The _____ button on the toolbar allows you to rearrange records by the values contained in a specific table column.

16. Ordering a table by the contents of two or more columns requires using the _____ dialog box.

17. Once the fields for a multiple field sort are defined, click the _____ _____ button on the toolbar to execute the sort.

18. Click the _____ _____ button in the Find dialog box to locate the next occurrence of the search string.

19. The shortcut command for the Find operation is _____ + _____ .

20. Use the _____ _____ _____ button on the toolbar to select records that meet certain criteria.

COMPUTER EXERCISES

The following exercises require the Paymast table, from the Projects database which you created in Session 1.

1. Perform the following tasks on the Paymast table.
   a. Sort the table by last name.
   b. Sort the table by YTD gross.
   c. Sort the table by employee ID.
   d. Sort the table by last name and first name. List the table.
   e. Use the Find command to find all the employees who have a gross pay of $2975.00.
   f. Use the Find command to find all the employees who have a pay rate of $7.75.

2. You are responsible for maintaining the database for a student club to which you belong. This database, named Club, contains information about each student member. Name and address information as well as interests and graduation dates are stored in the table. The Club database table has the following structure:

Field	Field Name	Type	Width
1	ID	Text	4
2	Date	Text	8
3	Last	Text	15
4	First	Text	12
5	Init	Text	1
6	Locaddr	Text	25
7	Loccity	Text	15
8	Locstate	Text	2
9	Loczip	Text	5
10	Locphone	Text	13
11	Homaddr	Text	25
12	Homcity	Text	15
13	Homstate	Text	2
14	Homzip	Text	5
15	Homphone	Text	13
16	Year	Text	1
17	Graddate	Text	15
18	Major	Text	3
19	Clubmajor	Text	1
20	New_ren	Text	1
21	Memb	Text	1
22	Publ	Text	1
23	Social	Text	1
24	Bus	Text	1

The fields with the Loc prefix contain data about the local address of the member, whereas the Hom prefix refers to the home data.

The Year field contains a number that designates the year in school (1 = freshman, 2 = sophomore, 3 = junior, and 4 = senior).

a. Create the primary key (the ID field) that will be used to list records from the table.

b. Add yourself as a member.

c. Use the Datasheet window to display each member's first and last name on-screen, together with his or her graduation date.

INTERNET EXERCISES

1. Examine Access 97 Product Assistance provided by Microsoft.

    a. Access the Microsoft Web page with your browser (http://www.microsoft.com).

    b. Click the Products button at the top of the Web page, and then choose Access 97 for Windows 95 from the list of products.

    c. Click the Visit the Microsoft® Access 97 for Windows® 95 Website link in the Contents pane on the left side of the page.

    d. Click the Enhancements and Assistance link on the page that appears.

    e. Click the Access 97 Assistance link on the page that appears.

    f. Print the first Web page.

Relating Tables, Modifying Table Structures, and Generating Reports

After completing this session, you should be able to:

➤ Set relationships between tables

➤ Change the structure of a table

➤ Control data input

➤ Search for and replace fields in a record

➤ Delete records

➤ Generate reports

Isabel wants to show Alice some safeguards that Access provides to protect a user from inadvertently deleting a record from one table that is needed by another table. She also wants to show Alice how to set up one-to-many relationships between tables.

Isabel also wants to show Alice how to control what kind of data can be entered in a table. Alice will be able to control the type of data that can be entered in a field as well as set up input masks that control how data is entered in a field.

Finally, Isabel and Alice want to be able to make use of the Report Wizard feature of Access to create reports that can be run at any time.

This session shows you how to set up relationships between tables, to change the structure of a table, limit the type of data that can be entered in a field, search and replace fields in a record, and delete records. Finally, it introduces the Report command, which allows you to generate a printed report.

RELATING TABLES   Tools, Relationships

You have probably noticed that there are several tables in the Membership database. All of these tables are related to one another. Table 3.1 shows these relationships.

When dealing with related tables, the relationships among the tables are referred to as a parent/child relationships. The **parent table** is the table used as the main table for a relationship. The **child table** is the related table and often has several records for each record in the parent table. The record pointer in the parent table controls how records are accessed in the child table. Table 3.2 describes the kinds of relationships you can establish between parent and child tables.

Table 3.1   Relationships Among the Membership Database Tables

Table Name	Table Function
Membership Data	This is the principal data table. It contains information about each member. Its identifying field is Membership ID Number. The Amount Due field holds credit information about each member. When a member charges a purchase, the total amount of the purchase is added to this field. Only one of these records can exist for each member.
Inventory Transactions	This table is used to record each purchase a member makes. Each member can have multiple records in this table. This table also holds the item number of each purchase, and the same item can appear many times in this table.
Inventory Data	This table contains one record for each inventory item. It keeps track of the vendor, items on hand, and so forth. The same vendor can appear many times in this table.
Inventory Purchases	This table holds information about inventory purchases made from suppliers. There can be multiple occurrences of vendors, but only one occurrence for each inventory item.
Supplier Data	This table holds information about suppliers. There can only be one record for each supplier.

Table 3.2 Parent/Child Table Relationships

Type of Relationship	Effect of Relationship
One-to-one	One child record for each parent record (rarely found in the real world)
One-to-many	Several child records for each parent record (most common type)
Many-to-many	Several parent records with matching keys in the child, and several child records with matching keys in the parent

Referential Integrity

A child record could possibly be entered in a table without a corresponding parent record. A child record without a parent record is called an **orphan record.** The Membership database, for example, should not allow for non-members making credit purchases, since only members are permitted to charge purchases to their Health Club account. Therefore, before a person can make a purchase, there must be a corresponding record in the Membership Data table. Such a requirement is called **referential integrity.**

Permanent and Transient Links

Access provides two methods of linking tables: permanent links and transient links. A **permanent link** is established using the Relationships command and is always in effect after it has been defined. A **transient link** is defined using the query-by-example feature of Access and is a temporary link.

Hands-On Exercise: Linking Two Tables

1. **Open the Membership database and click on the Tables tab of the opening dialog box.** Do not open any data tables.

2. **Establish a relationship with the Inventory Transactions tables.**

Tools	Click to open the Tools menu.
Relationships . . .	Open the Relationships window.
Relationships	Click to open the Relationships menu.
Show Table . . .	Click to open the Show Table dialog box (Figure 3.1). You use this dialog box to select tables to be related.

3. **Select the tables.**

MEMBERSHIP DATA	Double-click to select this table.
INVENTORY TRANSACTIONS	Double-click to select this table.
[Close]	Click to close the Show Table dialog box. You should now see the Relationships window with two table boxes visible (Figure 3.2).

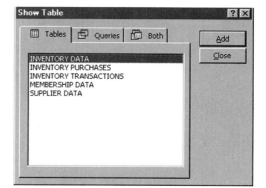

Figure 3.1
The Show Table dialog box.

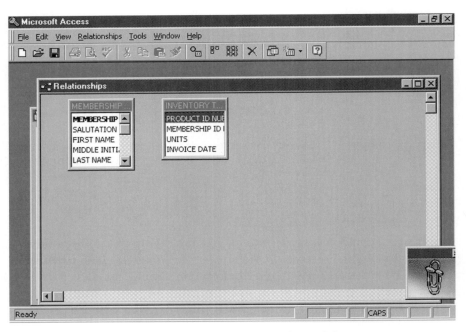

Figure 3.2
The Relationships window used to set up relationships between tables.

4. Set up the relationship between the Membership Data and Inventory Transactions tables.

Click and drag   Click Membership ID in the Membership Data box, and drag to the same field in the Inventory Transactions box. The Relationships dialog box shown in Figure 3.3 appears. It allows you to indicate the types of constraints to place on the relationship.

Enforce Referential Integrity

Click to activate this option. Your finished Relationships dialog box should look like Figure 3.4. This option prevents records appearing in the child table that do not have an occurrence in the primary table.

          Click to create the relationship. Your Relationships window should look like Figure 3.5.

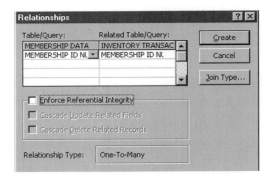

Figure 3.3
The Relationships dialog box.

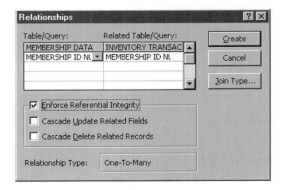

Figure 3.4
The completed Relationships dialog box.

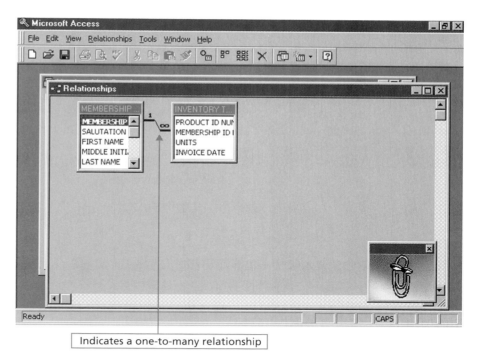

Indicates a one-to-many relationship

Figure 3.5
The Relationships window showing the relationship created between the Membership Data and Inventory Transactions tables.

5. **Make the change permanent.**

    Click to close the Relationships window. The alert box shown in Figure 3.6 appears.

    Click to save the data and return to the Database window.

Reinforcing the Exercise

1. Referential integrity prohibits deleting a parent record when a child record exists for that parent.
2. Most often, tables have a one-to-many relationship with records in another table.
3. A link can be permanent or transient.
4. A permanent link is established using the Relationship window.
5. Tables containing a relationship must share a common field that is used to link data from one table to another.

Figure 3.6
The alert box prompting you about saving the changed relationship data.

MODIFYING A TABLE STRUCTURE or Design

You can change a table structure by using the table design window. Access provides two ways of opening the table design window.

- Click the Design command button in the Database window.
- Click the View button on the Datasheet window toolbar.

Adding a Field to a Table Structure

As you work with an existing table, you may decide that you need an additional field to hold a new type of data. You can do this easily by using the Insert Row button in the table design window.

TIMELY TIP

> If you are making changes in several fields of a table structure, it is a good idea to save the table after each field has been changed. This allows Access to keep track of which field in the old structure belongs to the changed table in the new structure. If you don't do this, Access does not know where to put the data and simply erases any fields about which it has doubts.

Hands-On Exercise: Adding a Field

Alice wants to insert a region field following the Zip field in the Membership Data table.

1. **Open the Membership database if necessary.**

2. **Open the Membership Data table.**

MEMBERSHIP DATA

Double-click the table name to activate the Datasheet window.

Click to maximize the Datasheet window (Figure 3.7).

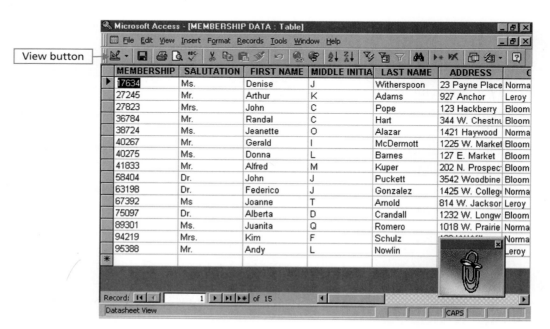

Figure 3.7
The Membership Data table displayed in the Datasheet window.

3. Activate the table design window.

     Click to open the table design window (Figure 3.8).

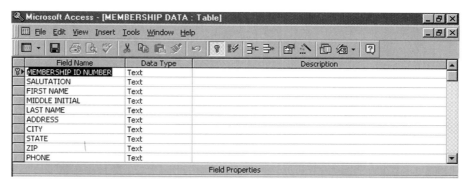

Figure 3.8
The structure for the Membership Data table.

4. Insert the new field.

PHONE   Click the Phone field.

     Click this button on the toolbar to open a blank field definition in the table structure (Figure 3.9).

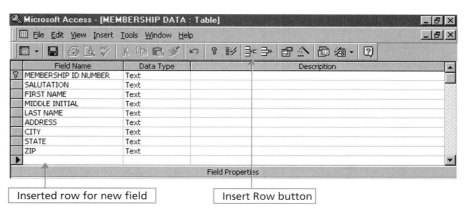

Inserted row for new field   Insert Row button

Figure 3.9
The table with a blank row inserted for the new field definition.

5. Enter the structure of the new field.

Type the field name: **REGION**

(ENTER)   Press to accept the name and the default Text data type.

6. Enter the field size.

Field Size   Click to the right of the 50 in the Field Size cell of the Field Properties box at the bottom of the table design window.

(BKSP)   Press twice to delete 50.

Type a new field width: **1** The table structure should now look like Figure 3.10.

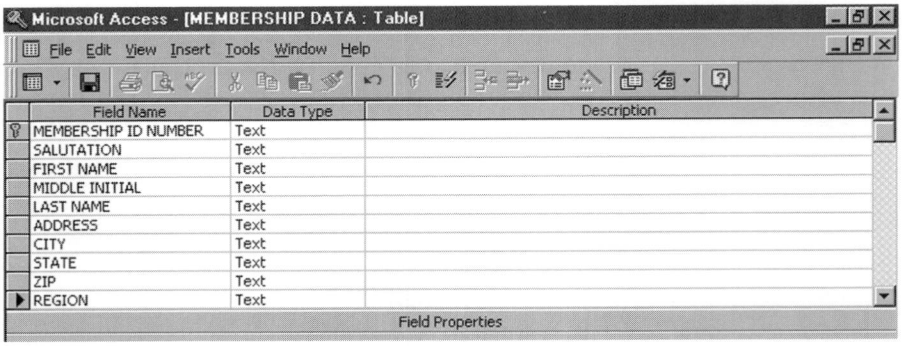

Figure 3.10
The Region field added to the table structure.

7. **Save the structure to disk.**

 Click this button (on the menu bar) to decrease the size of the table design window.

 Click this button to close the table design window. A dialog box asks if you want to save your changes to the Membership Data table.

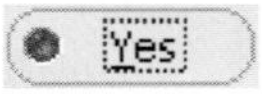

Click to save the changes to table structure to disk and (or press (ENTER)) return to the database window.

8. **Open the Membership Data table.**

MEMBERSHIP DATA Double-click the table name to open the Datasheet window.

 Click the scroll arrow on the horizontal scroll bar to see the blank Region field (Figure 3.11).

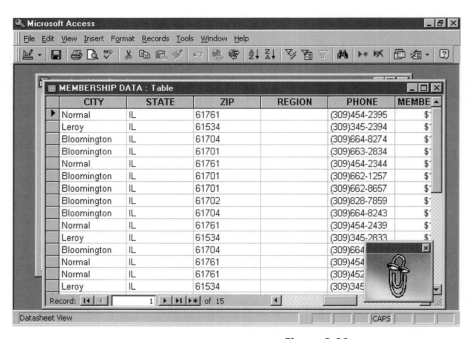

Figure 3.11
The Membership Data table with the inserted Region field.

Reinforcing the Exercise

1. Once you have defined a table, you can make changes to it within the table design window.

2. You add fields by clicking the Insert Row button.

3. An inserted field is blank.

Controlling Data Entry and Display

You may want to exercise more control over how Access enters and later displays data in a table. For example, suppose you want to control the range of characters entered in the Region field, automatically include parentheses and a dash in the Phone field and slashes in all date fields, and force uppercase characters in the State field. You also want date fields to show month names rather than numbers. Access allows you to control how data is entered via the Field Properties box of the table design window. Access uses the Format, Input Mask, Default Value, Validation Rule, and Validation Text cells of the Field Properties box to control data input and display (Figure 3.12).

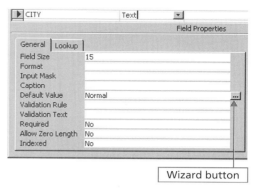

Figure 3.12
The Field Properties box.

Format

The Format cell allows you to use a predefined format for a data type and enables you to design your own display format. (This section concentrates on the predefined display formats.)

Input Mask

An **input mask** specifies how data is entered and displayed in the text box. Table 3.3 describes the **input mask characters** you can enter in the input Mask cell to control how data is entered. If you do not want to enter the input mask manually, you can click the Wizard button that appears on the right edge of the Input Mask cell, and Access offers to build the mask for you via the **Input Mask Wizard.** Once the Input Mask Wizard appears onscreen, you can select the desired entry.

Default Value

The Default Value cell, as the name implies, allows you to specify the default value for a field or control. This default value is entered in a field when you create a new record. For example, in the City field, you might specify the city most likely to occur (Normal, in this application). You can either accept this value or enter a new name/value when you add records to the table.

   If you are using a numeric field, the entry can be a numeric constant or a formula.

Validation Rule/Validation Text

A **validation rule** is an algebraic or logical expression that Access evaluates when data is entered for this field. You can enter the validation rule in the Validation Rule cell manually or use the Wizard button to open the

Table 3.3   Input Mask Characters

Character	Description
0	Requires a digit (0–9) entry; no plus (+) and minus (−) signs allowed.
9	Digit or space entry required; no plus and minus signs allowed.
#	Digit or space entry not required; blank positions are converted to spaces; plus and minus signs are allowed.
L	Letter (A–Z), entry required.
?	Letter (A–Z), entry optional.
A	Letter or digit, entry required.
a	Letter or digit, entry optional.
&	Any character or space, entry required.
C	Any character or space, entry optional.
.,:;-/	Decimal placeholder and thousands, date, and time separators. (The characters depend on the settings in the International section of the Microsoft Windows Control Panel.)
<	Causes all characters that follow to be converted to lowercase.
>	Causes all characters that follow to be converted to uppercase.
!	Causes input mask to fill from right to left, rather than from left to right, when characters on the left side of the input mask are optional. You can include the exclamation point anywhere in the input mask.
\	Causes the character that follows to be displayed as the literal character (for example, \A is displayed as A).

expression builder. The **validation text** is part of the text that appears in an alert dialog box if the data entered in the field does not conform to the expression entered in the Validation Rule cell. The maximum length of the validation text you can enter in the Validation Text cell is 255 characters.

If the validation rule is omitted, no validation takes place, so it makes no sense to enter anything in the Validation Text cell (no error could trigger the display of the text).

These two entries are typically used in conjunction with one another to make it easier for you to enter valid data in a table cell. You could, for example, use this feature to make certain that a user enters a value in the Region field that is between 0 and 7. If no value is entered, or the value entered is greater than 6, the error message would appear. As the default, Access does not allow a null value (empty field) to be stored in a field.

When you are using some of the features from the Field Properties box as discussed above, Access requires that you save the current table design before making any other changes to the table structure.

Hands-On Exercise: Controlling Data Entry in Selected Fields

Alice wants to make the following changes to the Membership Data table:

*   Place Normal as the default for the City field.

*   Change all data entered in the State field to uppercase.

*   Use the Input Mask Wizard to create an input mask for the Zip field.

*   Create a validation rule that allows only the values 1 through 6 to appear in the Region field. If a value outside that range is entered, an appropriate error message is displayed.

*   Use the Input Mask Wizard to create an input mask for the Phone field.

*   Use the Format cell to control the display of the Membership Expiration Date field and create an input mask for the date slashes.

1. **Open the Membership database and the Membership Data table if necessary.**

2. **Activate the table design window.**

 Click to open the table design window to make changes to the table structure.

3. **Enter a default value for the City field.**

Data Type   Click the Data Type cell of the City field. The Field Properties box for that field appears at the bottom of the table design window.

Default Value   Click this cell of the Field Properties box.

Type the default value: **Normal**

The Field Properties box should look like Figure 3.13.

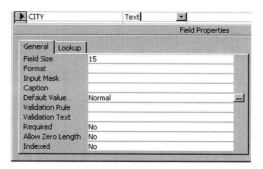

Figure 3.13
The Field Properties box for the City field.

4. Change the State field data to uppercase.

Data Type   Click the Data Type cell of the State field. The Field Properties box for that field appears at the bottom of the table design window.

Input Mask   Click this cell of the Field Properties box.

Type: **>LL**   The greater-than symbol (>) indicates that all letters that follow are to be changed to uppercase. The *LL* entry indicates that two letters must be entered.

The Field Properties box should look like Figure 3.14.

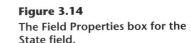

Figure 3.14
The Field Properties box for the State field.

5. Use the Input Mask Wizard to create an input mask for the Zip field.

Data Type   Click the Data Type cell of the Zip field. The Field Properties box for that field appears at the bottom of the table design window.

Input Mask   Click this cell of the Field Properties box.

Click to open the Input Mask Wizard dialog box. Access now prompts you to save the table (Figure 3.15).

Click to save the table. The Input Mask Wizard dialog box appears (Figure 3.16).

Zip Code   Click this entry.

Click to incorporate the input mask into the Field Properties box (Figure 3.17).

Figure 3.15
The Access dialog box requires you to save the table before making changes to the table via the Field Properties box.

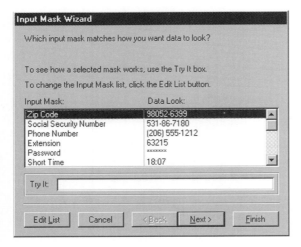

Figure 3.16
The Input Mask Wizard dialog box allows you to control data entry in a field.

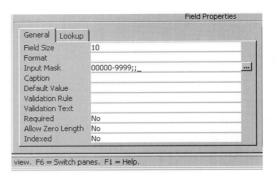

Figure 3.17
The Field Properties box for the Zip field.

6. **Create a validation rule to allow only the values 1 through 6 to appear in the Region field.** If a value outside that range is attempted, display an appropriate error message to the user.

Data Type Click the Data Type cell of the Region field. The Field Properties box for that field appears at the bottom of the table design window.

Validation Rule Click this cell of the Field Properties box.

Click to open the Expression Builder dialog box (Figure 3.18).

Type the first valid value: **1**

Click this button to make the word *or* part of the expression.

Type the next valid value: **2**

Click this button to make the word *or* part of the expression. Continue entering values through 6. Do not click the Or button after entering 6. The finished expression should look like Figure 3.19.

Click to place the expression in the Validation Rule cell.

Validation Text Click this cell of the Field Properties box.

Type: **Only the values 1 through 6 are valid.**

This is the text to be displayed if the region value is not a digit between 0 and 7. The Field Properties box should look like Figure 3.20.

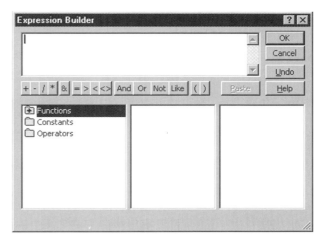

Figure 3.18
The Expression Builder dialog box opens when you click the Wizard button that appears to the right of the Validation Rule cell.

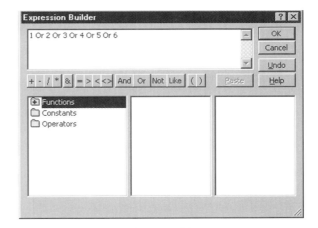

Figure 3.19
The completed Expression Builder dialog box.

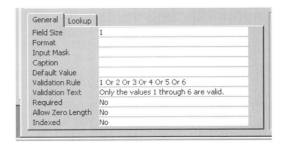

Figure 3.20
The Field Properties box for the Region field.

7. Use the Input Mask Wizard to create an input mask for the Phone field.

Data Type Click the Data Type cell of the Phone field.

Input Mask Click this cell of the Field Properties box.

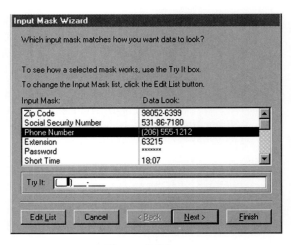

Figure 3.21
The Input Mask Wizard dialog box with the mask showing in the Try It text box.

... Click to open the Input Mask Wizard dialog box. Access prompts you to save the table.

● Yes Click to save the table. Access indicates that integrity rules have changed and asks if you want to apply the new rules to existing table data.

No Click to indicate that the rules do not apply (all of your existing Region fields are currently blank). The Input Mask Wizard dialog box appears.

Phone Number Click this entry.

Try It: Click this box. The Input Mask Wizard looks like Figure 3.21.

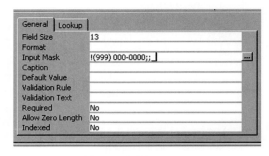

Figure 3.22
The Field Properties box for the Phone field.

Finish Click to incorporate the input mask into the Field Properties box (Figure 3.22).

8. Use the Format cell to control the display of the membership expiration date and create an input mask for the date slashes.

Data Type Click the Data Type cell of the Membership Expiration Date field.

Format Click this cell of the Field Properties box.

▼ Click this button in the Format cell. The list box shown in Figure 3.23 appears.

Medium Date Click to select this type of display. This entry appears in the Format cell.

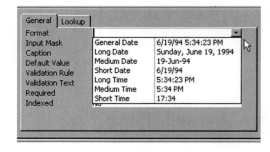

Figure 3.23
The available date formats appear in the Format list box.

Input Mask   Click this cell of the Field Properties box.

    Click this button in the Input Mask cell. Access prompts you about saving the table.

    Click to open the Input Mask Wizard dialog box (Figure 3.24).

Short Date   Click this entry.

    Click to incorporate the input mask. Your Field Properties should look like Figure 3.25.

9. **Return to the Datasheet window.**

    Click to return to the Datasheet window. Access prompts you about saving the changes to the table (Figure 3.26).

    Click to save the changes. Once the table is saved, the Datasheet window appears.

    Click the scroll arrow of the horizontal scroll bar until the Region field appears (Figure 3.27). Notice that the City field of the blank record has the default value of Normal entered. The Zip field entries all have trailing dashes.

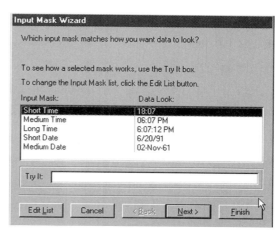

Figure 3.24
The Input Mask Wizard for the Date field.

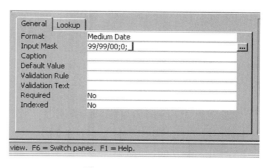

Figure 3.25
The Field Properties box for the Membership Expiration Date field.

Figure 3.26
The dialog box prompting you to save the table.

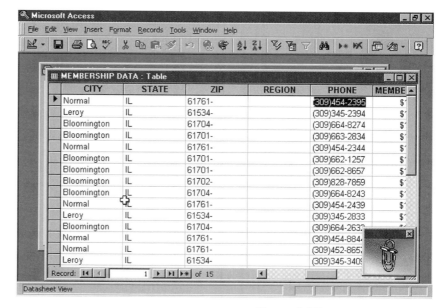

Figure 3.27
The datasheet incorporating the recent changes.

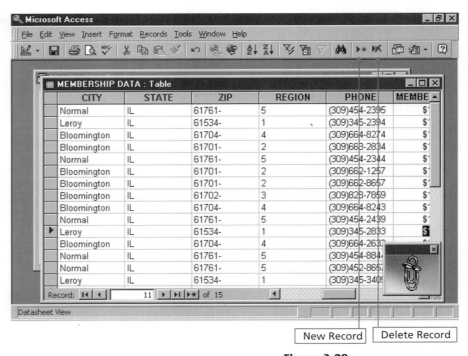

New Record   Delete Record

Figure 3.28
The table with the new region numbers.

10. **Enter the new region numbers shown in Figure 3.28.** Try to enter an invalid number; when you do and then try to move to another record, an alert dialog box similar to that shown in Figure 3.29 appears.

11. **Enter a new record with your name and address information, using the new data entry formats and displays.**

 Click to enter a record containing your individual, personal data. Use the value 22356 for your Membership ID number and 6 for your region. Notice that as you get to the fields with the input masks, those masks do not appear until you start to enter data in that field.

Figure 3.29
Alert dialog box with the error message created previously.

12. **Resize the Datasheet window and save the table.**

 Click to close and save the table.

TIMELY TIP

If you don't like the position of a field in the table structure, you can use a drag procedure to drag that field to the desired location. Follow these steps:

1. Select the field by placing the cursor in the gray border column and waiting for it to become a large right arrow.
2. Click. The field row appears in reverse video.
3. Click the border column box again and drag to the desired location.

Reinforcing the Exercise

1. The Field Properties cells control how data can be entered in a table.

2. You can select from predefined formats for entering data by selecting the Format cell.

3. The Default Value cell defines a specific value that is to be placed in a field automatically when a new record is added to the table.

4. The Validation Rule and Validation Text cells are used together to control what data can be entered and to display an error message if the correct data is not entered.

5. The Field Properties box supplies a number of Wizards that help you control how data is entered in a table.

REPLACING TEXT IN A TABLE   Edit, Replace

You already know how to make changes in a record via the Datasheet window. The Replace command also makes changes to a specific record or to all records within a table. Unlike the Datasheet window, however, the Replace command does not display a record before it is changed.

The Replace command functions much like a search-and-replace word processing command. Access searches for one character string in the selected field and, when it finds it, replaces it with another character string.

When you issue the Edit, Replace command sequence, the Replace dialog box appears as shown in Figure 3.30. You type the text you want to locate in the Find What text box, and then enter the replacement text in the Replace With text box. This command is especially useful if, for example, you misspell a frequently entered value for a field. You could easily locate every occurrence of *Blooomington* and replace it with the correct spelling of *Bloomington*.

The Replace command works similarly to the Find command covered in Session 2. You first move the cursor to the desired field and then issue the Replace command. You can also select the entire column.

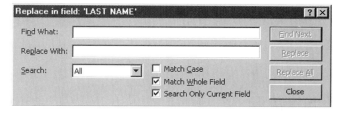

Figure 3.30
The Replace in Field dialog box. Last Name was selected in this case before the Replace command was executed.

DELETING RECORDS   Edit, Delete, ⬭DEL⬭, or ✖

From time to time, you will want to delete records from a database table. Clicking the Delete Record button accomplishes this task if you are in a table with a one-to-many relationship like the Inventory Transactions table. However, if you are in a table that demands referential integrity, an alert box appears when you issue the Delete Record command. This means that you cannot delete a parent record when there are child records in another table for that parent.

If you press the Delete Record button to delete a child record, a dialog box like that depicted in Figure 3.31 appears. It tells you that if you click the Yes button the record will be permanently deleted from the table.

Figure 3.31
The dialog box that appears when you issue the Delete Record command informing you that the operation cannot be undone later.

CREATING REPORTS

Data stored in a table is not worth much by itself; for the data to be useful in practical terms, it must be printed in report form. Session 1 introduced a method for simply producing listings of records in a table. This method, however, did not give you much control over how the information appeared on the report.

You can also click the left border cell of a record to select the entire record and then press (DEL) to delete a record from the table.

Access's Report feature provides much more flexibility in designing reports. The Report feature builds a **report template** that contains the report format, headings, and fields to be included in the report.

Building a Report by Using a Report Wizard

When you create a report you can design it yourself or use **Report Wizards** to help you. Using a Report Wizard is the easiest method and is the one you will use in this text. If a table does not have many fields, you can tell Access to put the report together and then make changes to the report template.

Hands-On Exercise: Using a Report Wizard to Create a Report

Alice now wants to use a Report Wizard to step her through the report-building process.

1. **Activate the Membership database, if necessary.**

2. **Build a report.**

    Click to open the Reports tab (Figure 3.32). There should be no reports currently listed in the tab.

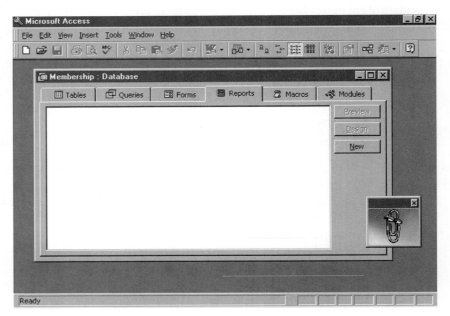

Figure 3.32
The Reports tab of the Database window.

Click this command button to open the New Report dialog box (Figure 3.33).

Click the down arrow of the text box. A listing of available tables appears (Figure 3.34).

INVENTORY PURCHASES

Click this table title.

AutoReport Tabular   Click to use this Report Wizard.

Click to build the report.

Click to enlarge the window. The report should look like Figure 3.35.

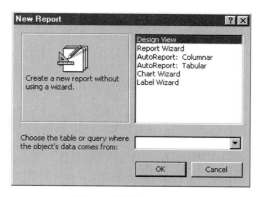

Figure 3.33
The New Report dialog box.

3. **Print the report.**

Click to print the report.

4. **View the report template.**

Click the Close button on the toolbar (Figure 3.35). The report design window appears (Figure 3.36).

5. **Save the report.**

Click the Save button on the toolbar to open the Save As dialog box.

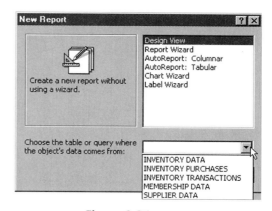

Figure 3.34
The listing of available tables.

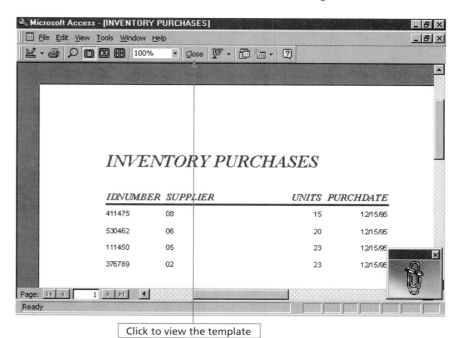

Click to view the template

Figure 3.35
The report created using the AutoReport Tabular Report Wizard.

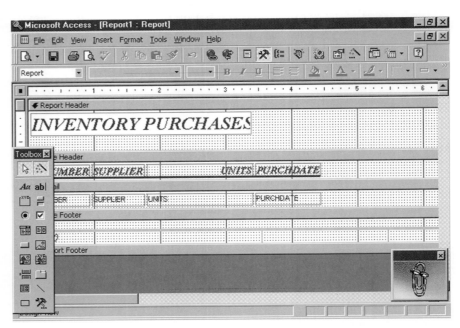

Figure 3.36
The report design window with
the specifications created by the
Report Wizard. The toolbox is in
the lower-left corner.

Type: **Inventory Purchases Report**

Click to save the file.

Click this button of the report design window.

Click the Close button to close the report design window
and return to the Database window. You should now see
the report name in the Reports tab (Figure 3.37).

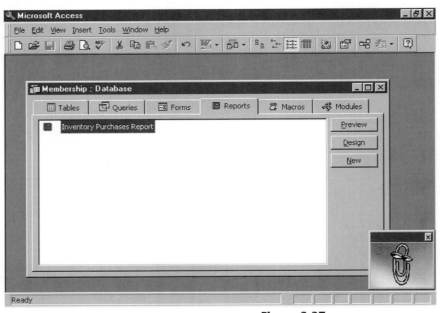

Figure 3.37
The Reports tab with the name
of the newly created report template.

Reinforcing the Exercise

1. You can access reports by using the Reports tab of the Database window.
2. You use the New Report dialog box to choose how you want to generate the report and to select the table that contains the data for the report.
3. A number of different reports can be generated using a Report Wizard.
4. The entries used to define the report are displayed in the report design window.

Working in the Report Design Window

The report design window has several main components (Figure 3.38). The toolbar has been dragged to the right side of the window.

Menu Bar and Toolbar

The menu bar is the standard Windows menu. It contains menu options relevant to the Access Report feature. The toolbars reside under the main menu and contain common Office 97 toolbar buttons.

Ruler

The ruler appears below the toolbars. As you position objects in the report, their location is shown in a dark shading on the ruler.

Report Layout

The report is displayed in **Design View** (Figure 3.38). It is divided into bands. All of the possible bands do not appear in the window unless they

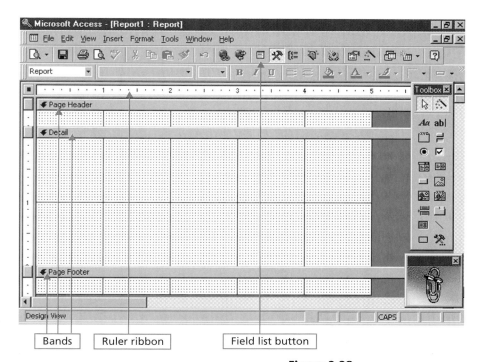

Figure 3.38
The report design window.

have been invoked via a menu or Report Wizard.

The **Report Header band** contains information that you want to appear only on the first page of the report.

The **Page Header band** defines the area at the top of each page of the report. It contains information such as page numbers, dates, and titles (such as company name, report name, and column headings).

The **Group Header band** contains information such as a group name or text that you want to have printed at the beginning of a group of records. This header is added automatically when you define the group field.

The **Detail band** contains the actual data from the database table. Text boxes that allow you to display fields from records are placed in this band.

The **Group Footer band** holds any identifying text and subtotals that have been generated by Access for a group of records.

The **Page Footer band** contains the text or data that is placed at the bottom of each page. The page number is automatically placed in this band by the Report Wizards.

The **Report Footer band** holds text and data that you want to have printed at the bottom of the last page of a report. A grand total number would, for instance, appear in this band.

Toolbox

The **toolbox** is a floating palette that is displayed whenever you open the Design View of a report (Figure 3.39). Clicking one of the palette buttons activates that tool, and the pointer then changes to the picture on the button. Table 3.4 describes the use for each tool.

If the toolbox is in the way of an area of the report design window that you want to access, you can either close the toolbox by issuing the View, Toolbox command sequence or by clicking its Close button, or you can drag the toolbox to another location onscreen.

Field List Box

The Field list box (Figure 3.40) displays a list of fields of the underlying table. The field(s) used in creating the primary key appear in bold. Fields can be dragged from the Field list box to the desired location in the report specification.

You can open the Field list box by clicking on the Field List button on the toolbar or by issuing the View, Field List command sequence. When you are finished using the field list, you can close it by clicking its Close button.

Figure 3.39
The report design toolbox.

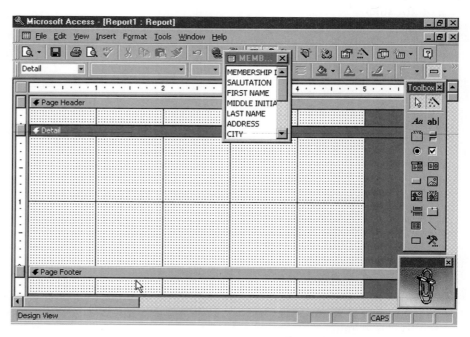

Figure 3.40
The Field list box displays the fields from the underlying table.

Table 3.4 The Report Design Toolbox

Icon	Name	Function
	Select Objects	Deselects an active tool and returns the pointer to its original shape and function. This is selected by default when the toolbox is displayed.
	Control Wizards	Toggles the Control Wizards on or off. These wizards can assist you in creating option groups, list boxes, and combo boxes.
	Label	Creates a box that contains constant text.
	Text Box	Creates a box that allows you to display and edit text data.
	Option Group	Creates an adjustable frame that you can use to hold toggle buttons, option buttons, or check boxes. Only one object can be selected and active at a time.
	Toggle Button	Creates a button that changes from on to off when clicked with the mouse.
	Option Button	Creates a round button that behaves the same as a toggle button.
	Check Box	Creates a check box that toggles on and off.
	Combo Box	Creates a drop-down combo box with a list from which you can select an item or enter a value in a text box.
	List Box	Creates a drop-down list box from which you can select. A list box is a combo box without the editable text box.
	Command Button	Creates a command button that, when selected, triggers an event that can execute an Access macro.
	Image	Creates a frame for displaying a picture on a form or report.
	Unbound Object Frame	Creates a frame for an OLE object for a form or report.
	Bound Object Frame	Creates a frame for a series of OLE objects on a form or a report.
	Page Break	Causes the printer to start a new page at this location in the report.
	Tab Control	Used to create a tabbed form with several pages.
	Subform/Subreport	Adds a subform or subreport to a main form or report. The subform or subreport must exist before you use this tool.
	Line	Draws a straight line that you can size and relocate. The size and color of the line can be controlled via the palette.
	Rectangle	Creates a rectangle that you can size and relocate. You can control various display attributes via the palette.
	More Controls	Allows you to embed a number of controls in a form.

Properties Sheet or Section Detail Sheet

The **Properties sheet** (Figure 3.41) shows the rules governing how a section or control (object) is being displayed. You can activate this feature in any of four ways:

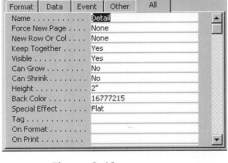

- Double-click a section or control

- Select a section or control and click the Properties icon of the toolbar

- Issue the View, Properties command sequence

- Open the context menu for the section or control (Figure 3.42) and then select the Properties option

Figure 3.41
The Properties sheet or Section Detail Sheet for the Detail band invoked by double-clicking the border.

Scroll Bars

The scroll bars let you move to a new location in your report layout. As you build your report, some areas may not be visible. Move to the desired area using the scroll bars.

One advantage of using Design View is that the printed report looks more or less like the onscreen template. This results in few or no surprises when you finally print the report. If you want to see exactly how the final product will appear, use the Print Preview feature, which you can open by clicking the Print Preview toolbar button.

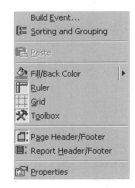

Redesigning a Report

When you are generating reports, the data is typically presented in some type of order (for example, primary key). Working within the report design window, you can place the report in order by fields other than the primary key.

Figure 3.42
The context menu opens when you click the right mouse button when the pointer rests on any object in the report.

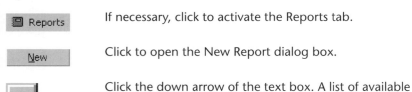

Hands-On Exercise: Building a Report

Alice wants to create a report based on the Membership Data table. She wants to try using a Report Wizard.

1. **Open the Membership database, if necessary.**

2. **Specify the Membership Data table as the underlying table for the report.**

	If necessary, click to activate the Reports tab.
Reports	
New	Click to open the New Report dialog box.
▼	Click the down arrow of the text box. A list of available tables appears.

MEMBERSHIP DATA

Click this table.

Report Wizard

Click to select the Report Wizard.

| OK |

Click to open the Report Wizard dialog box, which prompts you for the fields to include in the report you want (Figure 3.43).

3. **Specify the First Name and Last Name fields to be included in the report.**

FIRST NAME

Click this field name in the Available Fields list box.

| > |

Click this button to place the First Name field in the Selected Fields list box.

LAST NAME

Click this field name.

| > |

Click to place the Last Name field in the Selected Fields list box.

4. **Repeat step 2 to include the Address, City, State, and Zip fields in the report.** The Report Wizard dialog box should look like Figure 3.44.

| Next > |

Click to move to the next dialog box. Access prompts you to determine the grouping of records in the report.

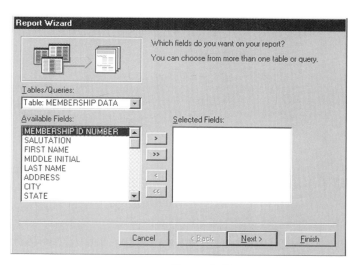

Figure 3.43
The first Report Wizard dialog box allows you to select the fields to be included in the report.

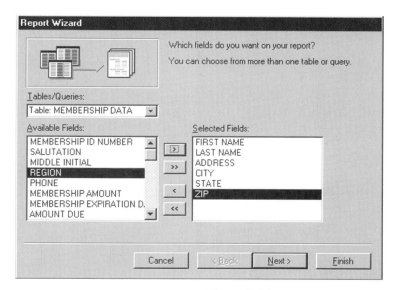

Figure 3.44
The fields to be included in the report are listed in the Selected Fields box.

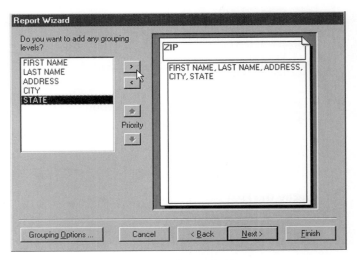

Figure 3.45
The grouping for the report is
determined.

5. **Specify that the records are to appear in zip code groupings.**

ZIP   Click this field name.

>   Click to decide the grouping. The Report Wizard dialog
                        box should look like Figure 3.45.

Next >   Click to proceed to the next dialog box (Figure 3.46),
                        which asks you to determine the order within the record
                        groupings.

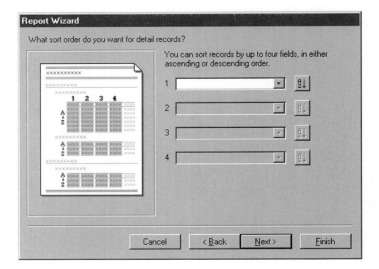

Figure 3.46
The Report Wizard dialog box
for determining the order within
the record groupings.

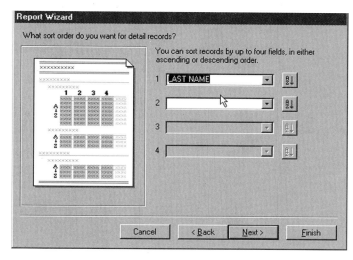

Figure 3.47
The completed Report Wizard
dialog box for determining the
order of the records within the
record groupings.

6. **Specify the order of the report as alphabetical order by name.**

      Click this button of the first field to invoke a listing of the field names.

LAST NAME   Click this field name in the list box. The dialog box should look like Figure 3.47.

      Click to see the next dialog box (Figure 3.48). Access now prompts you for the report style.

      Click to accept the defaults and go to the next dialog box (Figure 3.49). Access now asks you about the font styles to use in the report.

Figure 3.47
The completed Report Wizard
dialog box for determining the
order of the records within the
record groupings.

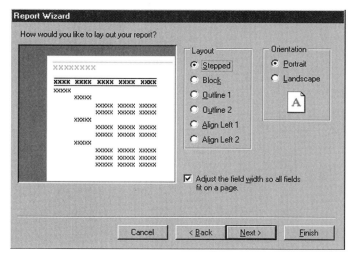

Figure 3.48
The various report style options.

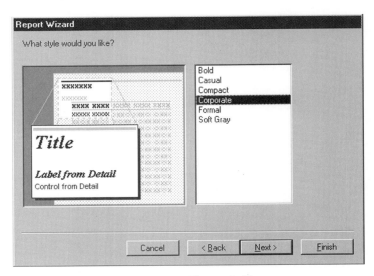

Figure 3.49
The Access report font styles available.

   Click to accept the defaults and go on to the next dialog box (Figure 3.50). Access now asks you if you want to use a report title that is different from the name of the table.

Type a new report title: **MEMBERSHIP NAME AND ADDRESS REPORT**

7. View the report.

Finish   Click to tell Access to prepare the report based on your specifications. When finished, it displays the Print Preview window for the generated report.

□   Click to maximize the Print Preview window.

   Click the down arrow button on the Zoom Control box to open the list box.

75%   Click this entry. The screen should look like Figure 3.51.

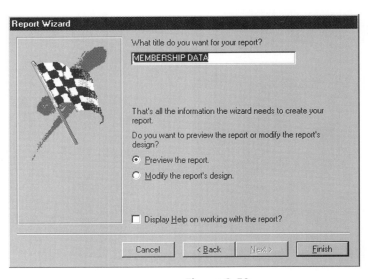

Figure 3.50
The default report title is the table name.

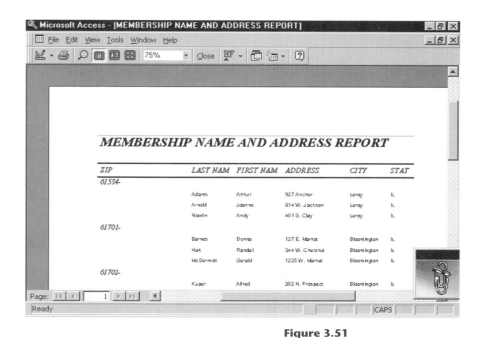

Figure 3.51
The report generated by the Report Wizard.

8. View the report template.

Click the Close button on the toolbar. The report design window shows the specifications that Access used for creating the report. Unfortunately, the toolbox may be in the way. Click the Design button.

9. If necessary, move the toolbox to the top of the window.

Click and drag   Click and drag the toolbox so it appears as shown in Figure 3.52.

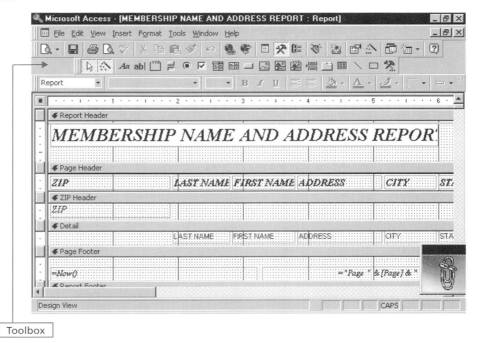

Toolbox

Figure 3.52
The Report design window with the toolbox at the top.

10. **Move the Page Header border down to the one-inch mark on the horizontal ruler.**

Drag   Click and drag to position the pointer on the upper portion of the Page Header band until the pointer turns into a vertical resize pointer. Drag the bar down just below the one-inch mark (Figure 3.53).

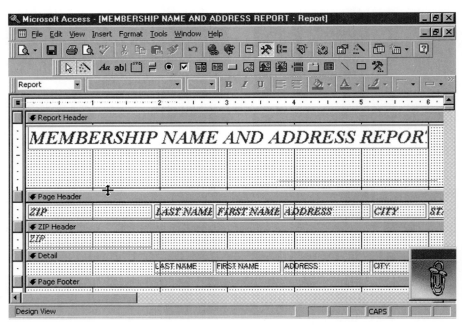

Figure 3.53
The moved Page Header band.

11. **Move the report title.**

Click   Click the title. A border appears.

Drag   Click and drag to move the report title to the location shown in Figure 3.54.

12. **Enter the organization's name as part of the header.**

Aa   Click the Label button in the toolbox. The pointer now appears as the Label icon.

Point and click   Move the pointer to the leftmost area of the Report Header band, above the report name, and click.

Type: **CIVIC CENTER HEALTH CLUB**

13. **Change the font size of the organization name to 20.**

Click   Click anywhere outside the text box to terminate text entry.

Click   Click the organization name to select it.

          Click the down arrow of the Font Size box on the toolbar. It currently has the value of 11.

20   Click to change the font size to 20 point.

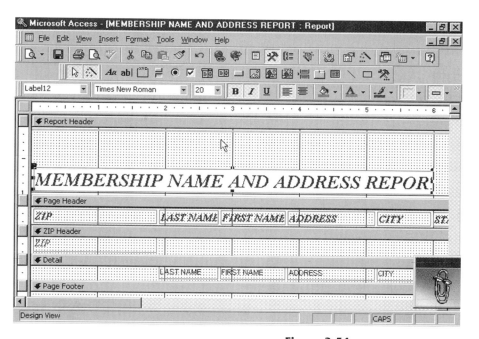

Figure 3.54
The new location for the report title.

14. Move the organization name.

Click and drag   Click on the lower-right selection handle, and drag until
your screen looks like Figure 3.55.

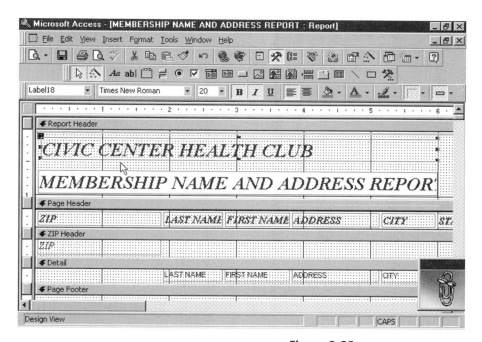

Figure 3.55
The inserted and resized organization name.

15. Center the new title in the Report Header band.

 Click the Center button on the toolbar to center the text in the selected box. You will have to use the arrows of the horizontal scroll bar to move the screen display.

16. Preview and print the report.

 Click to open the Print Preview window. The screen should look like Figure 3.56.

 Click to print the document.

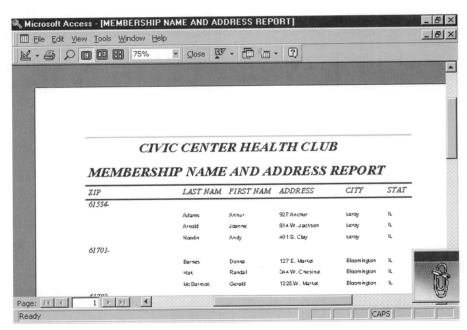

17. Save the report.

 Click to return to the report design window.

 Click to Save the report.

 Click to restore the report design window.

 Click to return to the Database window.

Figure 3.56
The report shown in the Print Preview window.

TIMELY TIP

If you inadvertently "misplace" a field or text box, reposition it by dragging it to the desired location in the report design window.

In addition to using an expression to assure that correct data is being entered in a field, you can also use the Lookup feature. The Lookup feature provides a list of valid data values that can be used for data entry. This list is obtained by using the items (values) that were entered when the value list of the Lookup field was created. This field is most easily created using the Lookup Wizard from the Data Type selection list. Creating a Lookup field for the Region field requires the following steps:

1. Select Lookup Wizard as your Data Type

2. Decide how the data will be entered for the Region field where you want to enter the values. You can choose to have data entered from a data source like a query or table, or to enter it manually.

3. Decide how many columns you will need, and in this case, enter the region numbers (1 through 6 each in a different cell).

4. Finish the process.

Once you have finished, your Lookup box should look like that shown in Figure 3.57. Save the changes and view the Datasheet. When you click the region field, an arrow appears. Click the arrow and, a list of the valid values appears (Figure 3.58) from which the field value can be selected.

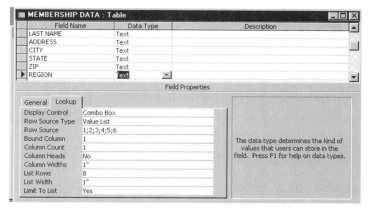

Figure 3.57
The completed Lookup box for the Region field with the valid values shown in the Row Source text box.

Figure 3.58
The acceptable values for the Region field generated by the Lookup command.

Reinforcing the Exercise

1. When you use a Report Wizard, you are stepped through a number of dialog boxes that help to define the report.
2. The Report Wizard automatically uses the table name as the title of the report.
3. Once you have generated a report by using a Report Wizard, you can change that report in the report design window.
4. Each item that appears in a report is an object that you can select and manipulate.
5. A selected object has selection handles that you can use to resize or move the object.

SESSION REVIEW

Access allows you to indicate how tables should be related to each other. A table can have a one-to-one, one-to-many, or many-to-many relationship. A table that has referential integrity allows only one parent record for each child record.

Access allows you to make changes to the structure of a database table. You can add, delete, and rearrange fields in the table structure. You can also control how data will be entered in a table by using the Properties sheet of a field. The Properties sheet allows you to enter default values in a field, control how data in a field will be displayed, create an input mask for making data entry easier, validate data as it is being entered and display an error message if it is incorrect, and force any data entered to uppercase.

The Replace command changes several records for a field one at a time, in accordance with selection criteria.

You can delete a record or a group of records from a table by selecting the desired record(s) and then pressing ⌐DEL⌐. Access verifies that you want the record(s) deleted before it physically removes the record(s) from the table.

The Reports feature of Access lets you format a report from information contained in a table. The report design window provides a number of bands for you to use in describing the report, including bands for specifying report and column headings and any fields you want to print. A band also generates totals for any numeric fields.

KEY TERMS AND CONCEPTS

child table 6–64	many-to-many relationship 6–65	referential integrity 6–65
Design View 6–83	one-to-many relationship 6–65	Report Footer band 6–84
Detail band 6–83	one-to-one relationship 6–65	Report Header band 6–83
expression builder 6–72	orphan record 6–65	report template 6–80
Group Footer band 6–84	Page Footer band 6–84	Report Wizard 6–80
Group Header band 6–83	Page Header band 6–83	toolbox 6–84
input mask 6–71	parent table 6–64	transient link 6–65
input mask characters 6–71	permanent link 6–65	validation rule 6–71
Input Mask Wizard 6–71	Properties sheet 6–86	validation text 6–72

SESSION QUIZ

Multiple Choice

1. Which of the following is not a relationship that can be established between parent and child tables?
   a. one-to-one
   b. many-to-one
   c. one-to-many
   d. many-to-many

2. Which of the following is used to control how data is to be entered/displayed for a table?
   a. Control sheet
   b. Properties sheet
   c. Display sheet
   d. none of the above

3. A Report Wizard lets you:
   a. establish a report title
   b. print column headings
   c. number each page
   d. print totals
   e. all of the above

4. Which of the following report bands is automatically used to hold page numbers?
   a. Page Header band
   b. Detail band
   c. Page Footer band
   d. none of the above

5. Which of the following statements is true about the input mask for a field?
   a. It can be used to allow only uppercase characters.
   b. It can be used to allow only numeric digits.
   c. It can be used to allow only alphabetic characters.
   d. It can be used to allow optional or required characters.
   e. all of the above

True/False

6. The Input Mask Wizard creates an input mask for frequently used data type fields.

7. You can physically remove a record from a table by pressing DEL.

8. The Report Wizards allow you to create only two types of reports.

9. The Validation Rule cell is typically used in conjunction with the Validation Text cell of the Field Properties box.

10. The toolbox makes controlling data entry much easier.

SESSION REVIEW EXERCISES

1. A _____ record can have one or more child records.

2. The _____ table is the related table.

3. A _____ relationship will have one child record for each parent record.

4. A child record without a parent record is called an _____ record.

5. A _____ link is established using the Relationships command.

6. Clicking the _____ _____ button adds a field to the table definition.

7. The _____ _____ of the table's Field Properties box, when used, contains characters that control how data is entered.

8. The _____ _____ cell of the table's Field Properties box contains an entry that will automatically be placed in a record field whenever a new record is added to the table.

9. The _____ _____ can be used to make it easier to build a validation rule.

10. The _____ character is used to indicate that uppercase characters must be used.

11. The _____ and _____ entries of the Field Properties box are typically used in tandem.

12. The _____ command provides the ability to search for one value in one field of all records and change that value.

13. The _____ _____ toolbar button is used to delete a table record.

14. _____ _____ prohibits you from accidentally deleting a parent record when a child record for that parent still exists.

15. A report _____ is built and stored in the database any time that a report is defined to Access.

16. A _____ _____ is used to build a report easily.

17. The _____ tab of the Database window is used to select an existing report or to start the report definition of a new report.

18. The _____ _____ _____ of the report design window is used for inserting a text object in an existing report.

19. A report is made up of a number of different _____ bands.

20. The _____ _____ displays a listing of fields of the underlying table.

COMPUTER EXERCISES

1. Perform the following tasks using the Paymast table, which you created and used in Sessions 1 and 2.
   a. Look at the structure of the database records.
   b. Make certain that only an uppercase letter is entered for the middle-initial field.
   c. Make certain that only the department values of 10, 15, and 20 are used. Generate an error message if some other value is entered. (*Note:* Use " around the department numbers to indicate character data and not numeric value.)
   d. Delete record 5.
   e. Create the report shown in Figure 3.59 and print it using the Report Wizard. Resize the heading box and center it.
   f. Create another report using the Report Wizard, and include the same fields as the prior report. Specify that it is to be sorted by department number. Use the report name of Payroll Register Report by Department. What differences did you find in the two reports?
   g. Add the following fields to the Paymast table: Address, City, State, and Zip. Give each field an appropriate length.
   h. Use the Datasheet window to fill in data that you make up for each record.

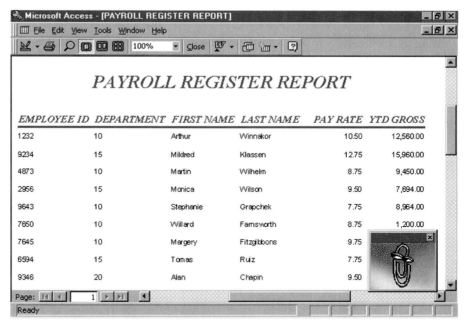

Figure 3.59
The payroll register report.

2. This exercise requires the Inventory Data table of the Membership database. For information about the structure of this table, use the Design Structure command.

   Create a report template, Inventory Listing Report, that looks like Figure 3.60. (*Hint:* Be sure to resize the fields so that they are the same as in the figure. Resize the fields as you did when you centered the headings: drag the handles of a border box to the desired location.)

INVENTORY LISTING REPORT

ID NUMBE	ITEM	SIZE	PRICE	SUPPLIE	REORDER	OPTIMUM
112276	CHICAGO BULLS SWE	LARGE	27.50	01	25	200
138800	CHICAGO BULLS SWE	EX-LARGE	29.95	01	25	180
115022	HOCKEY STICK		50.00	03	20	150
153064	BEGINNER'S RACKET		75.00	04	10	75
153361	JORDAN SPECIAL	10	125.00	02	20	75
111450	CROSS TRAINER	11M	85.00	05	20	75
113068	CROSS TRAINER	10M	85.00	05	15	75
118588	HOCKEY PUCK		7.50	03	15	
142679	FIGURE SKATES	7N	89.95	03	10	

Figure 3.60
The inventory listing report.

INTERNET EXERCISES

1. Use the Access Assistance Library.
   a. Access the Microsoft Web page with your browser (http://www.microsoft.com).
   b. Click the Products button at the top of the Web page, and then choose Access 97 for Windows 95 from the list of products.
   c. Click the Visit the Microsoft® Access 97 for Windows® 95 Website link in the Contents pane on the left side of the page.
   d. Click the Enhancements and Assistance link.
   e. Click the Access 97 Assistance link.
   f. Click the More Access Assistance link near the bottom of the page.
   g. Browse through the links displayed on the Microsoft Access 97 Assistance Library page. Visit any links that relate to generating reports.
   h. Go back to the Assistance Library page.
   i. Print the Web page.

SESSION 4

Creating Queries and Forms

After completing this session, you should be able to:

➤ Create queries for a database

➤ Create forms for a database

➤ Create a subform

➤ Create a chart

 Isabel has asked Alice to build queries that will allow them to access information about the membership of the Civic Center Health Club and about the outstanding balances that members have with the gift shop.

Isabel also wants to build one or more forms that can be used for displaying data and for updating records in membership tables. She especially wants to create a form that displays data about a specific member as well as information about that individual's recent purchases at the gift shop.

In this session you will learn how to create queries with and without Query Wizards. You will also learn how to create and customize forms and subforms. Finally, you will use a Form Wizard to create a chart.

QUERIES

A **query** is a set of instructions that specifies how Access should organize or change your data. Session 2 introduced entering an elementary query by using the Filter feature. You used this type of query to sort records in a table. This section introduces you to creating queries by using Query Wizards, dynasets, and the query design window. You will use these queries to ask questions about your data and build models of the information. Queries can use fields from one or more database tables. With queries you can display data, enter data in a database table, generate a report, rearrange fields in a table, update a database table, or limit the fields that a user can access.

The most common and easiest way to create queries is by using **Query Wizards.** You can also custom design your own query by using the query design window.

Dynasets

When you finish creating a query, Access displays the results in a **dynaset,** which contains the fields you specified in the query and provides a view of data contained in the database table(s) you specified. You can use a dynaset just as you would a database table to display, enter, and edit data. The difference is that, when you use a dynaset, you can work with several fields from several different tables instead of only one table. Any changes that you make to the fields in a dynaset are automatically included in the records of the underlying tables.

When you have finished using a dynaset and close it, it no longer exists in memory. Access allows you to save instructions governing the query that defined the dynaset and then reuse those query statements later. You can also save the dynaset to a table, but the data in that table is not updated when you make changes to the tables used as input to the original query.

Creating a Query

You begin creating a query by selecting the Queries tab of the Database window (Figure 4.1). If you had created and saved any queries, they would be displayed on this tab.

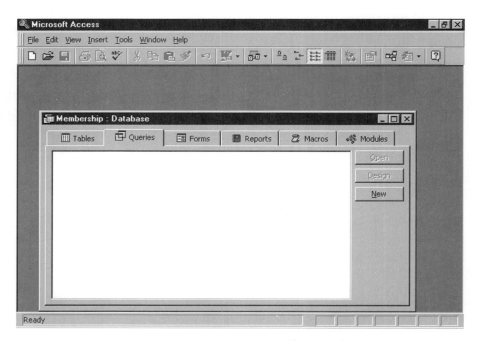

Figure 4.1
The Queries tab of the Database window.

Your next step is to click the New command button to display the New Query dialog box (Figure 4.2). You use this dialog box to indicate how you want to create the query. If you want to build the query yourself, you select Design View. (You will explore this option later in this session.) The other four options are Query Wizards:

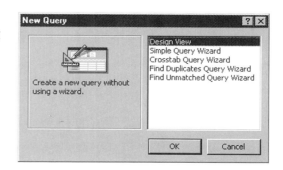

Figure 4.2
The New Query dialog box.

- The Simple Query Wizard creates a query based on questions answered in dialog boxes.

- The Crosstab Query Wizard displays data in a compact, spreadsheet-like format.

- The Find Duplicates Query Wizard creates a query that finds duplicate records in a single table or query.

- The Find Unmatched Query Wizard finds records in one table that have non-related records in another table.

You will be using the Simple Query Wizard to build your first query.

 Hands-On Exercise: Building a Query with a Query Wizard

Alice and Isabel want to include fields from the Membership Data table in a query that they will use to determine the amount each member owes.

1. **Open the Membership database.**

2. **Activate the Queries tab.**

3. **Start building the query.**

 Click to open the New Query dialog box (Figure 4.3).

Simple Query Wizard

Click this entry to indicate that you want a Query Wizard to help you build the query.

 Click to open the first Simple Query Wizard dialog box (Figure 4.4), which prompts you for the table(s) and fields you want to include in the query.

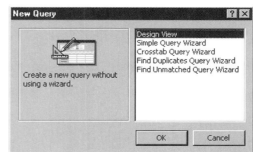

Figure 4.3
The New Query dialog box.

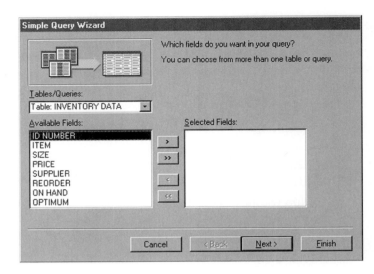

Figure 4.4
The Simple Query Wizard dialog box prompting you for the table(s) and fields you want to include in the query.

4. **Select the table for the query.**

 Click the down arrow of the Tables/Queries list box to get a listing of tables and queries (Figure 4.5).

MEMBERSHIP DATA

Select this table. The fields contained in that table now appear in the Available Fields box (Figure 4.6).

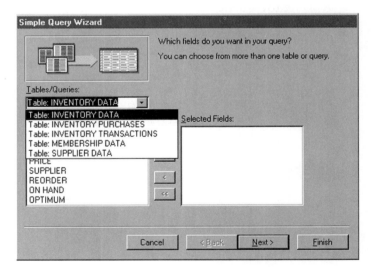

Figure 4.5
The Tables/Queries list box.

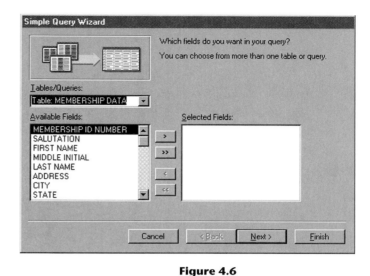

Figure 4.6
The fields contained in the Membership Data table appear in the Available Fields box.

5. **Select the fields to be included.**

FIRST NAME Click this field name.

Click to move the field to the Selected Fields box.

LAST NAME Click this field name.

Click to move the field to the Selected Fields box.

ADDRESS Click this field name.

Click to move the field to the Selected Fields box. Continue by adding the City, State, Zip, Phone, and Amount Due fields to the Selected Fields box. The completed dialog box should look like Figure 4.7.

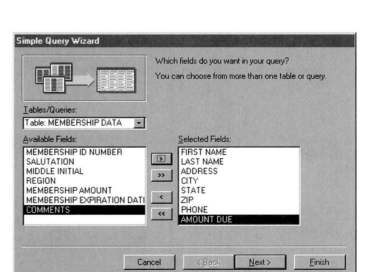

Figure 4.7
The completed dialog box for including selected tables and fields in the query.

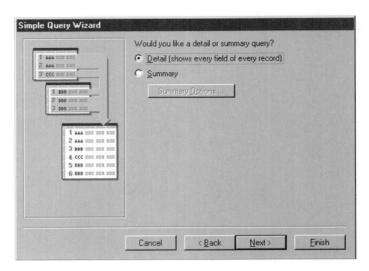

Click to proceed to the next Simple Query Wizard dialog (Figure 4.8), which asks you what type of report you want.

Figure 4.8
This dialog box lets you determine whether you want a detail or summary report.

Accept the Detail option and proceed to the next dialog box (Figure 4.9), which prompts you about the name to use for the query. The default name is the name of the first table you selected.

6.   Enter a different name for the query.

Type: **Amount Due Query**

Click to build the query. Access displays the dynaset for this query.

Click the right arrow of the horizontal scroll bar until the Amount Due field appears. The dynaset should look like Figure 4.10.

Figure 4.9
You use this dialog box to name the query.

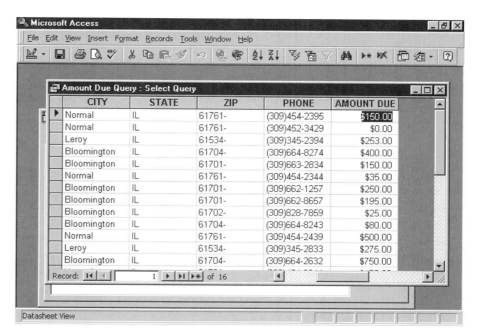

Figure 4.10
The dynaset.

7. **Examine the query in the query design window.**

 Click to switch to query design (Figure 4.11).

8. **Close and save the query.**

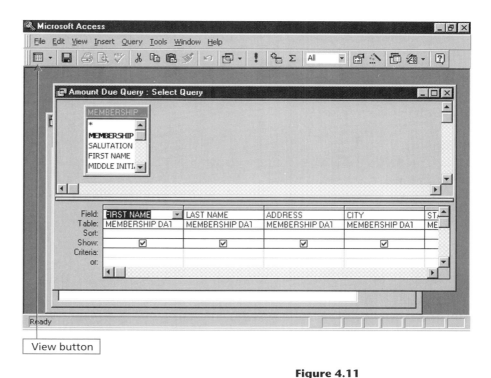

Figure 4.11
The query design window with the QBE entries used to create the query.

Reinforcing the Exercise

1. The Queries tab of the Database window lists any queries that have been created.

2. Click the New button of the Queries tab to start the process of creating a query.

3. You can use Query Wizards to speed the process of creating a query.

4. The records included in a query are placed in a dynaset table.

The Query Design Window

The query design window displays the specifications you established for the query you created. It does not contain data. At the top of the window is a fields list box for each table you included in the query. At the bottom of the window is a **QBE (query-by-example) grid.** You can use the QBE grid to control which fields are to appear in the dynaset as well as how fields are to be sorted, whether or not a field is to be displayed, and any criteria to use in including fields in the dynaset. The following sections describe each cell of the QBE grid.

Field

The names of the fields to include in a query are specified in the **Field cell.**

Table

The name of the table from which the field is obtained is specified via the **Table cell.**

Sort

The **Sort cell** displays a list box with the options Ascending, Descending, and (not sorted). This cell allows you to determine the order that fields appear in the dynaset. The order of fields in the QBE grid is important when you want to sort on multiple fields. Access starts with the leftmost field as the primary key and moves one field to the right for the secondary key field and so on in the sort order.

Show

You use the **Show cell** to determine whether or not a field is to be displayed in the dynaset. Fields with a check mark (√) in the Show cell appear in the dynaset, whereas fields with a blank cell do not appear. Both types of fields can be used to control the records that appear in the dynaset.

Criteria

In the **Criteria cell,** you enter any selection criteria for including records in the dynaset for a specified field. After you finish entering the expression and press (ENTER), Access examines it and displays the expression using standard Access syntax. For example, if you type Normal, Access adds quotation marks and displays it as "Normal".

The selection criteria you enter in the Criteria cell can include **relational operators,** which are listed in Table 4.1. If you don't include an operator, Access assumes the equal sign (=). For example, if you enter Normal in the City field, Access interprets that as the expression CITY = 'Normal'.

Table 4.1   Relational Operators

Operator	Description
<	Less than
<=	Less than or equal to
=	Equal to
>=	Greater than or equal to
>	Greater than
<>	Not equal to

When a query requires examining several fields, the selection criteria for the fields must be linked with the **logical operators** shown in Table 4.2.

Table 4.2   Logical Operators

Operator	Description
Not	The opposite of this expression must occur for this action to take place.
And	This condition requires that both conditions be true before any action will be taken.
Or	This condition requires that only one of the conditions be true for the action to be taken.
( )	Parentheses group relations together. If nested parentheses are used, Access evaluates an expression by starting with the innermost set and working outward.

In addition to using relational and logical operators, Access also supports the operators shown in Table 4.3. The operators give you tremendous flexibility in querying database tables.

Table 4.3   Other Operators

Operator	Description
Is	Used with Null to determine whether a value is Null or Not Null (whether a field is empty or not empty).
Like	Determines whether a string value begins with one or more specified characters. You must use the wildcards * and ? for this to work properly, for example, Blo*.
In	Determines whether or not a string value is in a list of values, for example, In("IL", "IA", "MN", "IN").
Between	Determines whether a numeric value lies within a range of values, for example, Between 1 and 6.

Table 4.4   Examples of String Searches

Expression	Task Performed
<=02/03/95	Matches dates on or before February 3, 1995.
<=G	In a character field, finds all records that start with "A" through "G" in a case-sensitive field.
*john	Matches records that include "john" somewhere in the field.
<>IL	Matches records that do not have the contents "IL".
Like "University*"	Matches records that include text beginning with "University". The * is the wildcard.

Access also allows you to use string searches, such as those shown in Table 4.4.

The Criteria cell may be too small to display a long criteria formula you might want to review. You can use the Zoom command ((SHIFT) + (F2)) to open the Zoom window to examine the criteria formula (Figure 4.12).

You execute the query by clicking the Run button on the toolbar. Access then displays the dynaset for the query (Figure 4.13).

Figure 4.12.
The Zoom window used for examining a long criteria specification.

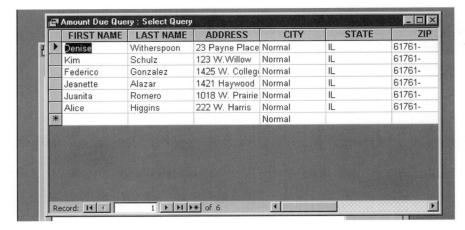

Figure 4.13
The dynaset containing all Normal records.

Hands-On Exercise: Modifying QBE Entries

Alice wants to modify the existing QBE entries to include those records that are in Normal or Leroy.

1. **If necessary, open the Amount Due query, and then open the query design window.**

2. **Enter query criteria.**

Criteria   Click the Criteria cell of the City column.

Type the name of the first city to be included: **Normal**

Or   Click the Or cell beneath Normal.

          Notice that double quotation marks appear around Normal.

Type the name of the second city: **Leroy**

          The query design window should look like Figure 4.14.

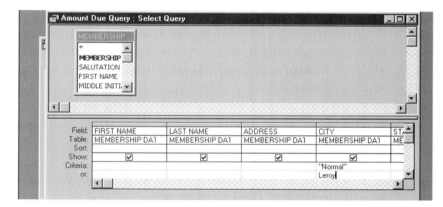

3. **Run the query.**

          Click to run the query. The dynaset shown in Figure 4.15 appears. Only Normal and Leroy records are included.

Figure 4.14
The completed QBE entries.

Figure 4.15
The dynaset for the Normal and Leroy records. The Higgins record was added in a prior example. Your output will include your record.

4. Print the results of the query.

       Click to print the dynaset.

5. Sort by last name and print.

       Click this button on the toolbar to return to Design View
                           and the query design window.

Sort   Click the Sort cell in the Last Name column.

       Click the down arrow to display the sort options.

Ascending   Click to select ascending order for the sort.

       Click to run the query. The dynaset should appear sorted
                           by last name (Figure 4.16).

6. Get rid of the city criterion.

       Click to return to the query design window.

Drag   Click and drag to select the *Normal* criterion.

DEL   Press to erase the *Normal* criterion.

Drag   Click and drag to select the *Leroy* criterion.

DEL   Press to erase the *Leroy* criteria.

**7. Enter criteria to locate those records with an amount due of greater
       than $250.**

                           Click the right arrow on the horizontal scroll bar until the
                           Amount Due field appears.

Criteria   Click the Criteria cell of the Amount Due field.

Type the criterion to locate records with an amount due greater than $250: **>250**

                           The completed QBE entries should look like Figure 4.17.

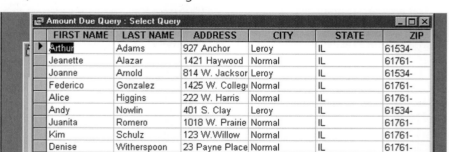

Figure 4.16
The selected records sorted by
last name.

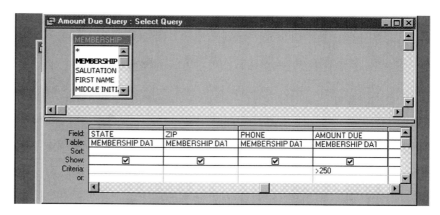

8. Run the query.

 Click to create the dynaset with the desired records.

 Click the right arrow of the horizontal scroll bar until the Amount Due field appears (Figure 4.18). Only those records with an amount due greater than $250 appear in alphabetical order. The zero amount is automatically included (new record row) for any record that might be added.

Figure 4.17
The QBE entries for obtaining all records with an amount due greater than $250.

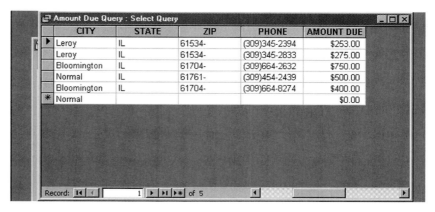

9. Exit the query without saving the changes.

 Click the Close button on the dynaset window. Access displays a dialog box asking if you want to save changes to the query (Figure 4.19).

 Click to exit without saving any changes.

Figure 4.18
The dynaset with those records containing an Amount Due value greater than $250.

Figure 4.19
The Access dialog box prompting you about saving changes to the query.

Reinforcing the Exercise

1. The Criteria cell in a QBE grid dictates the field contents of those records included in the dynaset.
2. The Run button tells Access to execute the query and create the dynaset.
3. The Sort cell of a field indicates the order to be used for records in the dynaset.
4. You use relational and logical operators in the Criteria cell.
5. If you enter no relational operator in the Criteria cell, Access assumes it is the equal sign.

Query Calculations on Groups of Records

You may want to generate summary totals for groups of records within a table or totals for all of the records. Decisions are often made on this type of summarized data. Making calculations based on table values requires creating a query that employs Access's **SQL aggregate functions.** The term *aggregate* indicates that these functions are used against *groups* of records. Table 4.5 summarizes these functions.

Invoking an aggregate function is a two-step process:

1. Add a Total cell to the QBE grid by clicking the Totals button on the toolbar.
2. Click the down arrow in the Total cell to get a listing of the SQL aggregate functions, and then click the one you want to use.

Table 4.5   SQL Aggregate Functions

Function	Description
Group By	Specifies the field on which to sort and develop the level break
Sum	Totals the values in a field
Avg	Averages the values of a field
Min	Determines the smallest value in a field
Max	Determines the greatest value in a field
Count	Determines the number of values in a field (no null values included)
StDev	Determines the statistical standard deviation of the values in a field
Var	Determines the statistical variation of the values in a field
First	Determines the value of the field of the first record
Last	Determines the value of the field of the last record

Hands-On Exercise: Generating Subtotals

Alice wants to generate summary totals as well as counts of records for each zip code in the Membership Data table. For this exercise, you should have the Membership database window active. You will be building your own query without relying on a Query Wizard.

1. Open the query design window to begin designing your own query.

| Queries | Click to activate the Queries tab of the Database window. |

| New | Click to activate the New Query dialog box. The Design View entry should be selected by default. |

| OK | Click to open the Show Table dialog box over the query design window (Figure 4.20). |

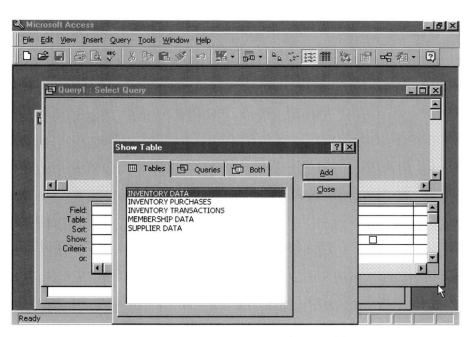

Figure 4.20
The Show Table dialog box with the query design window in the background.

MEMBERSHIP DATA

Click to select this table

| Add | Click to add this table name to the top of the query design window. |

| Close | Close the Show Table dialog box. The query design window should look like Figure 4.21. |

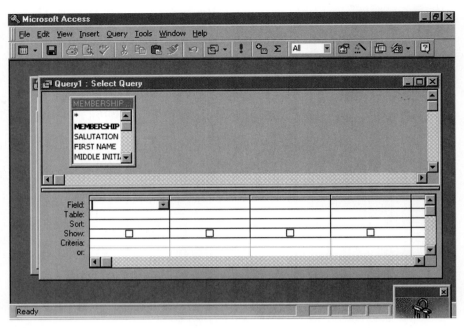

Figure 4.21
The query design window for a query based on the Membership Data table.

2. **Select fields from the Membership Data table.**

      Click the down arrow of the field list box scroll bar until the Zip field appears.

ZIP   Click the Zip field to place it in the first Field cell of the QBE grid.

      Go to the next field list box. Click the down arrow of the field list box scroll bar.

MEMBERSHIP ID NUMBER

     Click to place it in the second Field cell of the QBE grid.

      Click the down arrow of the fields list box scroll bar until the Amount Due field appears.

AMOUNT DUE   Click to place it in the third Field cell of the QBE grid. The query design window should look like Figure 4.22.

TIMELY   TIP

If you erroneously insert the wrong field in a query, you can delete that field by clicking the field name column of the QBE grid in which the incorrect field name resides, and then issuing the Edit, Delete Columns command sequence. The query field is now removed from the grid.

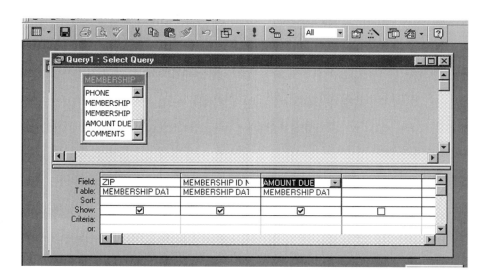

Figure 4.22
The completed QBE grid for the SQL aggregate query.

3. **Indicate to Access that totals are to be included.**

Σ

Click to insert a Total cell in the QBE grid.

Total

Click the right corner of the Total cell under the Member-ship ID Number Field cell. A list box of SQL aggregate functions appears (Figure 4.23).

Count

Click this option.

Total

Click the right corner of the Total cell under the Amount Due Field cell. A list box of SQL aggregate functions appears.

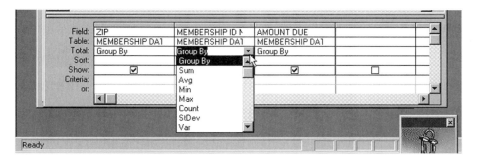

Figure 4.23
The list box for the SQL aggre-gate functions for summarizing numeric fields of a table.

Sum

Click this option. The QBE grid should now look like Figure 4.24.

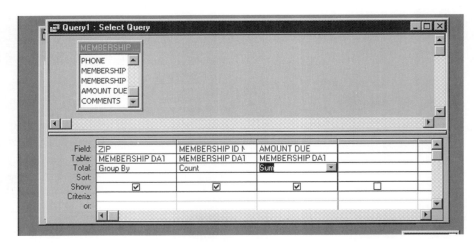

Figure 4.24
The completed query design window.

4. **Run the query.**

Click to run the query. A dynaset like that shown in Figure 4.25 appears. This dynaset shows zip code numbers, a count of members in each zip code, and the subtotal of the amount due for each zip code.

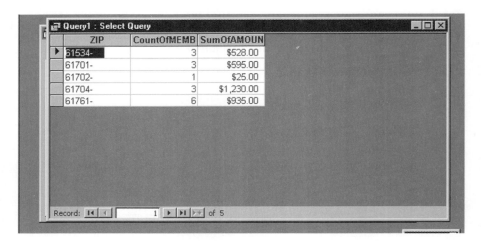

Figure 4.25
The dynaset for generating amount due subtotals by zip code. Your amounts may differ, based on the record added previously.

5. **Save the query.**

Click to return to the query design window.

Click to open the Save As dialog box.

Type: **Zip Code Total Query**

(ENTER)
Press to save the query. When you want to use this query, just click the entry in the Queries tab of the Database window and then click the Open button.

Click the Close button to return to the Database window.

Reinforcing the Exercise

1. You can build queries to report summary data such as totals and subtotals.
2. Click the Total button on the toolbar to include a Total cell in the QBE grid.
3. Use SQL aggregate functions to develop summary or group totals.
4. Use the SQL Count function to count records in a grouping.
5. Use the SQL Sum function to develop totals in a grouping.

 **On Your Own**

Create a number of queries using what you have learned.
- Find the names of the individuals whose membership expires before 1998 (<01/01/98).
- Find all individuals with first names that start with J (J*).
- Find all individuals who do not live in Bloomington (<>Bloomington).

VIEWING DATA BY JOINING TABLES

Isabel has asked you to create a goods sold report that has, for each item sold, the item's name, the supplier's name, and the number of units sold. Your Inventory Transaction table contains the item number and units sold. Your Inventory Data table can use the item number to find the corresponding item name for each item purchased. The supplier number for an item can be used to link to the appropriate supplier in the Supplier Data table. The Query feature of Access easily links these three tables so reports or queries for information from them can be contained, for example, in one query. You can create a query to display or print records from more than one table.

The first database table used in this application is the Inventory Transaction table. Figure 4.26 shows the structure for this table.

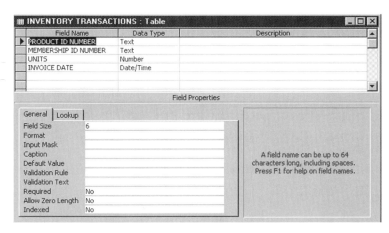

Figure 4.26
The structure for the Inventory Transaction table.

The second database table in this application is the Inventory Data table (Figure 4.27). The Supplier Data structure can be seen in Figure 4.28.

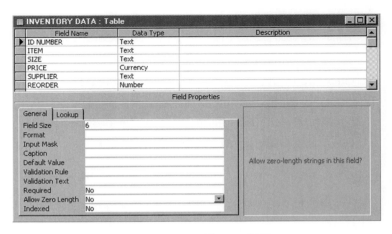

Figure 4.27
The structure of the Inventory Data table.

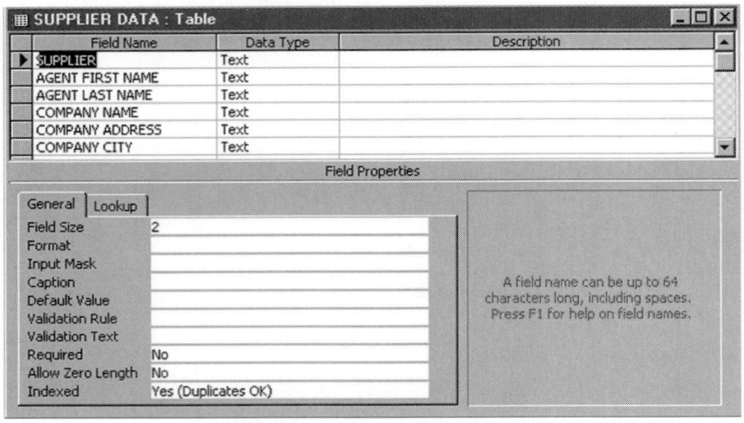

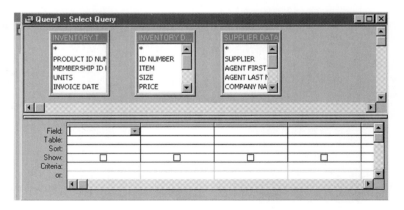

Figure 4.28
The structure of the Supplier Data table.

Tables to be linked must appear in the window above the QBE grid (Figure 4.29).

One limitation imposed by Access is that any two tables to be related or joined must share a **common field**. In this case, the PRODUCT ID NUMBER field of the INVENTORY TRANSACTIONS table is used to link to the INVENTORY DATA table via the ID NUMBER field. It is this field (with the same data) that lets Access link the two tables and display information from both tables in one line of a display or report.

Figure 4.29
Multiple tables specified in a Select Query operation.

The Supplier field is used to link the INVENTORY DATA and SUPPLIER DATA tables. This example shows the same named field linking tables. Using the same name in two tables allows you to make a linking application easier to understand but is not required by Access.

Linking tables together using Access is accomplished using a graphical approach. Simply click the field being used in one table and drag it to the corresponding field in another table in the upper window of the Query Design window (Figure 4.30). Once the tables have been linked, you can include any fields from any table in the query QBE grid.

If you want to delete a link or join between tables, position the mouse pointer to the line between the tables representing the link of two common fields, and right-click the mouse. Select the Delete command from the context menu.

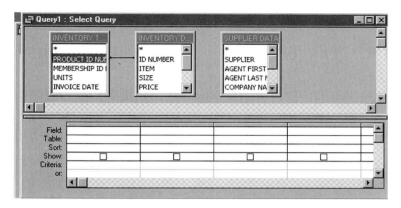

Figure 4.30
The INVENTORY TRANSAC-TIONS and INVENTORY DATA tables linked via a common field.

Hands-On Exercise: Link the Three Tables

This exercise requires you to have the Membership database window active on the screen.

1. **Indicate to Access that you want to build a new query and add the three tables.**

| Queries | Click this tab of the Database window. The query sheet appears on your screen. |

| New | Click to activate the New Query dialog box. It appears with the Design View option selected. |

| OK | Click the OK button to activate the QBE grid with the Show Table dialog box (Figure 4.31). |

INVENTORY TRANSACTIONS

Select this file.

| Add | Click to add the file name to the top of the Query Design window. |

INVENTORY DATA

Select this file.

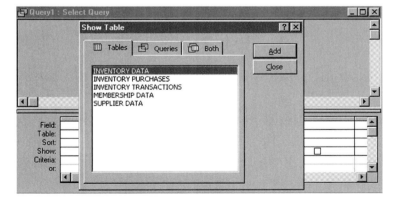

Figure 4.31
The Show Table dialog box above the QBE grid.

Add	Add the file name to the top of the Query Design window.

SUPPLIER DATA

Select this file.

Add	Add the file name to the top of the Query Design window.
Close	Close the Add Table dialog box. Your screen should now look like that depicted in Figure 4.32.

TIMELY TIP

If you inadvertently leave out a table, you can add that table to the query by issuing the command sequence Query, Show Table. The Show Table dialog box now appears, and the desired table can be added to the query specification.

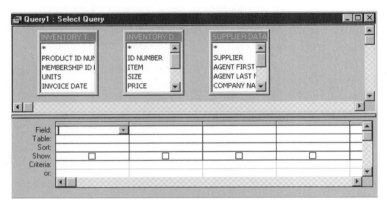

Figure 4.32
The three tables to be linked together appearing in the Query window.

2. **Link the tables based on the common fields.**

Drag

Drag the PRODUCT ID NUMBER field of the Inventory Transaction table to the ID NUMBER field of the Inventory Data table. A line appears that links the fields of the two tables, as shown in Figure 4.33.

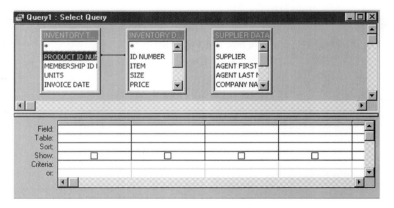

Figure 4.33
The talbes linked via the PRODUCT ID NUMBER and ID NUMBER fields

Drag	Drag the SUPPLIER field of the INVENTORY DATA table to the SUPPLIER field of the SUPPLIER DATA table. A line should now link the fields of the two tables. Your screen should now look like the top of Figure 4.34.

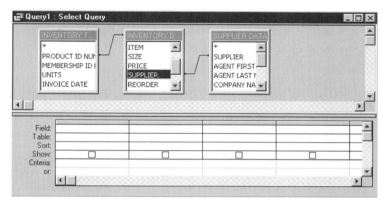

Figure 4.34
The links generated for the multitable join.

3. **Include a field from the Inventory Data table.**

ITEM	Double-click this field.

4. **Include a field from the SUPPLIER DATA table.**

COMPANY NAME	Double-click this field.

5. **Include a field from the Inventory Transaction table.**

UNITS	Double-click this field. Your Query Design window should now look like that depicted in Figure 4.35.

TIMELY TIP

If you forget to include a field in the QBE grid, drag it until your cursor is on the field that's just to the right of where you want the new field to go. When the mouse button is released, Access inserts the field to the left of the field in which the pointer resided.

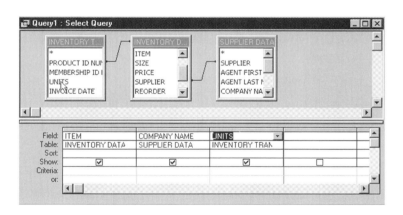

Figure 4.35
The completed QBE table for the multitable join.

6. **Display the dynaset for the query.**

    Click to run the query. The dynaset of the linked tables appears in the Datasheet window (Figure 4.36).

7. **Save the query using the name Inventory Link.**

CROSSTAB QUERIES

Crosstab queries are summary queries that display results in a spreadsheet-like format. These queries allow you to summarize data from one field and then cross-reference it with another field that has its data listed in the first column of the Crosstab query. Up to three fields can be used in sorted order for the cross-reference.

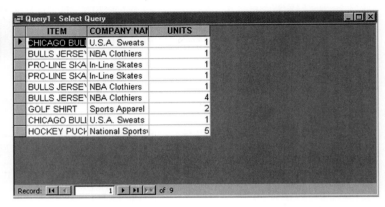

Figure 4.36
The dynaset generated via the linked tables.

Access provides a Crosstab Query Wizard to help you build such a query that is based only on one table or existing query. To incorporate data from more than one table, you must first build the join query to gather the fields and then specify that query as input to the Wizard.

Assume that you want to get a count of how many memberships have expired or will expire from the Membership Data table by region number.

Hands-On Exercise:
Counting Expired Memberships by Region

This exercise requires you to have the Membership database window active on the screen.

1. From the Query tab, click the New button.

    New

2. From the New Query dialog box, double-click the Crosstab Query Wizard. The first dialog box of the Crosstab Wizard appears.

3. Double-click the Membership Data Table. The second dialog box appears.

4. Double-click the Region field and then click the Next button (up to three fields can be specified here).

    Next >

5. Select the Membership Expiration Date field and then click the Next button.

    Next >

6. Click the Year entry to specify the time interval, and then click the Next button. The next dialog box has the MEMBERSHIP ID NUM-BER field selected in left box and the Count function selected in the right box (items that we want). You can select any field that is unique from one record to the next.

7. Click the Next button and the last dialog box appears.

8. Change the name of the crosstab to **Expiration by Region**. Click the Finish button, maximize the dynaset window and the results should look like Figure 4.37.

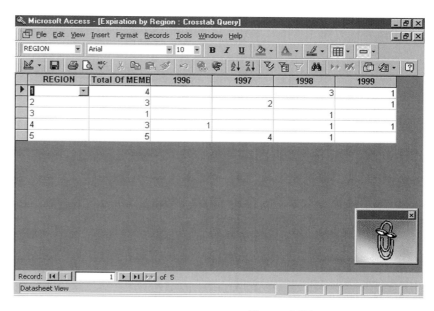

Figure 4.37
The query results shown in a spreadsheet-like format.

FORMS

Database applications have one common problem: The paper form that is frequently the source of the data does not resemble the screen you use to enter the data. For example, the Access Datasheet window shows the records and fields in a tabular format. Field names are often cryptic abbreviations that give a user little indication of what should be typed in each field. Another problem is that Access can display only a few fields onscreen at one time, even if the record contains a significant number of fields.

Access solves these problems by letting you create a customized data entry **form** that is similar to that of the source document. Such a source-document-oriented form allows you to include more text to make the form self-documenting. Figure 4.38 shows one such form.

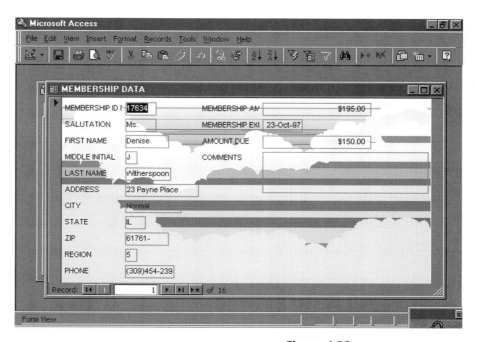

Figure 4.38
A data entry form created for the Membership Data table.

The Access **Form Wizards** make creating a form an easy task by prompting you through simple steps and then quickly generating the form for you. In the Forms tab of the Database window, you click the New command button to open the New Form dialog box (Figure 4.39). This dialog box requires that you select a table from a list box similar to the one you used to generate queries. You then indicate how the form is to be generated—manually or by using Form Wizards.

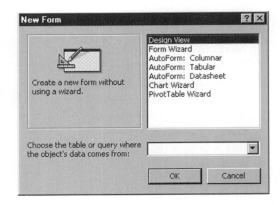

Figure 4.39
The New Form dialog box.

Hands-On Exercise: Creating a Form Using a Form Wizard

Isabel wants you to create a simple form like that shown in Figure 4.38 using the Form Wizard.

1. **If necessary, activate the Membership database.**

2. **Click the Forms tab of the Database window.**

3. **Create the form.**

              Click to open the New Form dialog box (Figure 4.39).

    AutoForm: Columnar

                       Click this option.

              Click the down arrow button for the Table list box to see a list of available tables and queries.

    MEMBERSHIP DATA Click this table name.

              Click to finish creating the form. Access displays the form shown in Figure 4.40. A speedbar for moving from record to record appears at the bottom of the form.

4. **Use the speedbar buttons to display the records on the form.**

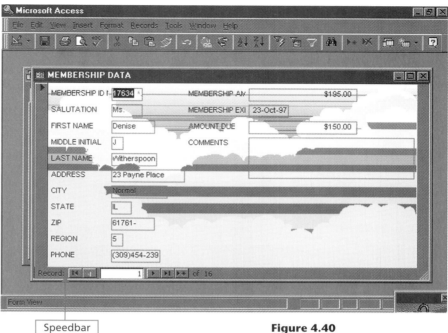

Speedbar

Figure 4.40
The completed columnar form
showing the contents of the first
record.

5. **Examine the form design window with the form definition entries.**

 Click to open the form design window (Figure 4.41).

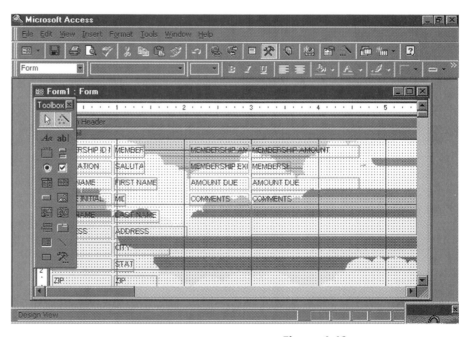

Figure 4.41
The form design window showing the underlying specifications
used in creating the form.

6. Save the form and exit.

Click to open the Save As dialog box.

Type: **Membership Form**

(ENTER) Press to save the form.

Click to close the form design window.

TIMELY   TIP

> As you can see, the form design window looks similar to the report design window. In this case, the field names are in boxes to the left of the field box that displays data when the form is active. The form design window also contains Header, Detail, and Footer bands, and the body of the form appears in the Detail band.

Reinforcing the Exercise

1. You access forms by using the Forms tab of the Database window.
2. Click the New button to begin creating a new form.
3. You can build a form on your own or with the help of a Form Wizard.
4. The created form contains a speedbar that you use to move from one record to another.
5. The form design window contains the title boxes and bands similar to a report design window.

Customizing a Form

Once you have generated a basic form, you can use it as a jumping off point to design your own form. You can choose which fields to include in the form and display additional descriptive data onscreen. You can also add additional controls that allow you to add many Windows-like features such as text, data fields, text boxes, list boxes, radio buttons, command buttons, or any other item that might appear on a form.

Before you can continue with the exercises in this session, you must establish relationships among the remaining tables in the database.

Hands-On Exercise: Relating the Remaining Tables

1. **If necessary, open the Membership database, and open the Tables tab of the Database window.**

2. **Open the Relationships window.**

Tools   Click to open the Tools menu.

Relationships   Click to open the Relationships window, which shows the
                          relationship that you created in Session 3 (Figure 4.42).

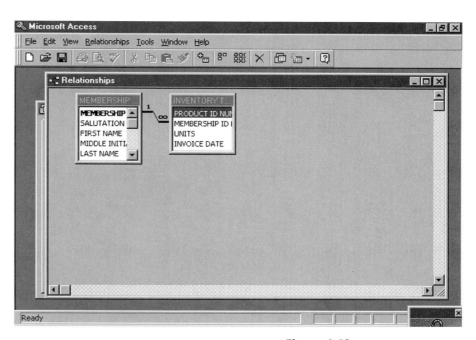
                          Click the Show Table button to open the dialog box
                          shown in Figure 4.43. The Show Table dialog box allows
                          you to define more relationships.

Figure 4.42
The Relationships window shows
the relationship between the
Membership Data and Inventory
Transactions tables that you al-
ready established.

3. **Add the other tables to the Relationships window.**

INVENTORY DATA   Click this table name to select it.

        Add   Click to add the table.

INVENTORY PURCHASES

                          Click this table name to select it.

        Add   Click to add the table.

SUPPLIER DATA   Click this table name to select it.

        Add   Click to add the table.

        Close   Click to close the Show Table dialog box.
                          Your Relationships window should now look
                          like Figure 4.44.

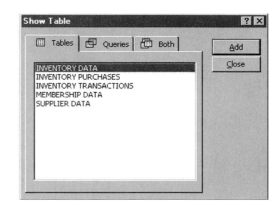

Figure 4.43
The Show Table dialog box al-
lows you to add tables to the
Relationships window.

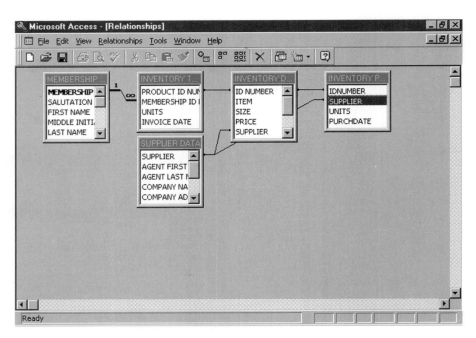

Figure 4.44
The Relationships window with the other database tables added to it.

4. **Establish the first relationship.**

Click and drag   Click the Product ID Number field of the Inventory
                        Transactions table and drag to the ID Number field of
                        the Inventory Data table. The Relationships dialog box
                        shown in Figure 4.45 appears.

          Click to create the relationship.

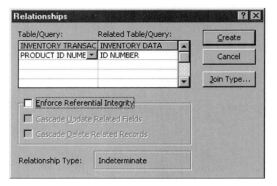

Figure 4.45
The Relationships dialog box for the first two tables.

5. **Repeat step 4 to relate the ID Number field of the Inventory Data
    table to the ID Number field of the Inventory Purchases table.** Then
    relate the Supplier field of the Inventory Data table to the Supplier field
    of the Supplier Data table. Now relate the Supplier field of the Inventory
    Purchases table to the Supplier field of the Supplier data table. The finished
    Relationships window should look like Figure 4.46.

6. **Close the Relationships window and save the changes.**

          Click to close the window. A dialog box appears asking if
                        you want to save the changes.

          Click to save the changes and close the window.

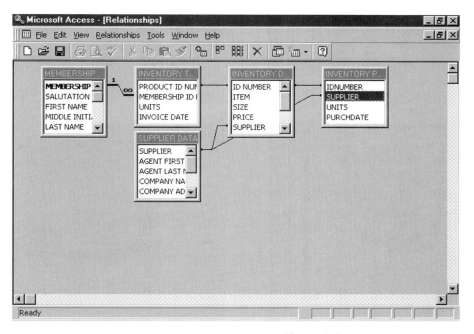

Figure 4.46
The established relationships for all of the tables.

 *On Your Own*

Note: Perform this exercise only after all of the tables have been related by the prior exercise.

Create a query using the Design View option. Include the following tables: Membership Data, Inventory Transactions, and Inventory Data.

- Once you have selected the tables, include the following fields from the specified tables:
  Membership Data:
    First Name
    Last Name
  Inventory Data:
    Item
    Price
  Inventory Transactions:
    Units
- Next to the Units field, enter the formula (PRICE) * (UNITS). Be sure to include the parentheses.
- When you run the query, you should see the calculated amounts.

Hands-On Exercise: Customizing a Wizard-Built Form

Alice wants to build a new form using a Form Wizard and then manually move fields to customize the form to suit her needs.

1. **If necessary open the Membership database and activate the Forms tab.**

2. **Activate the Form Wizard.**

| New | Click to open the New Form dialog box. |

| **Form Wizard** | Click this entry. |

| OK | Click to open the first Form Wizard dialog box (Figure 4.47). |

3. **Insert fields from the Membership Data table.**

 Click the down arrow in the Tables/Queries list box to see a list of tables and queries.

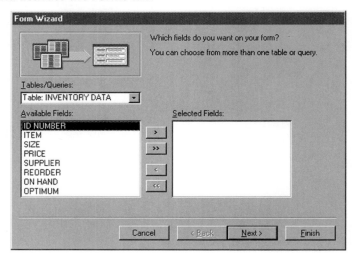

Figure 4.47
The Form Wizard dialog box for adding fields to the form.

MEMBERSHIP DATA

Click this entry. A list of the fields in this table appears in the Available Fields list box.

MEMBERSHIP ID NUMBER

Double-click to add this field to the Selected Fields box.

FIRST NAME   Double-click to add this field to the Selected Fields box.

LAST NAME   Double-click to add this field to the Selected Fields box. Continue adding the Address, City, State, Zip, Phone, and Amount Due fields. When you are finished, your Form Wizard dialog box should look like Figure 4.48.

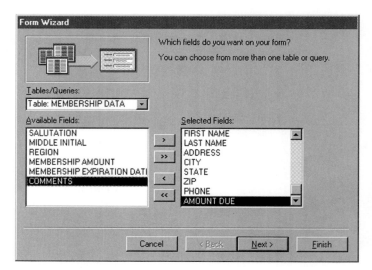

Figure 4.48
The fields from the Membership Data table to be included in the form.

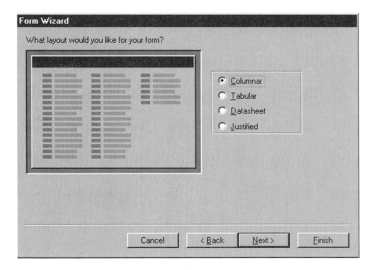

Figure 4.49
The second dialog box of the Form Wizard allows you to set the layout of the form.

4. Establish the layout and style of the form.

Next >	Click to proceed to the Form Wizard dialog box shown in Figure 4.49.
Next >	Click to accept the default Columns layout and proceed to the next dialog box.
Colorful 1	Select this style (Figure 4.50).
Next >	Click to proceed to the dialog box shown in Figure 4.51.

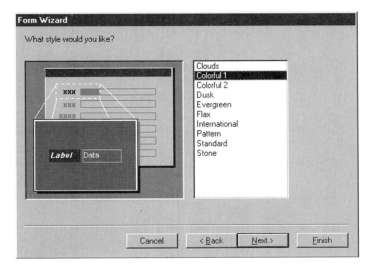

Figure 4.50
This Form Wizard dialog box allows you to choose the style of the form.

Figure 4.51
You use this dialog box to determine the title of the form.

5. Enter a new title.

Type a new title for the form: **Current Balance**

 Finish   Click to display the finished form (Figure 4.52).

6. View the form definition.

    Click to view the form definition in the form design window.

    Click to enlarge the window.

Drag   If necessary drag the toolbox to the bottom of the window. The form design window should look like Figure 4.53.

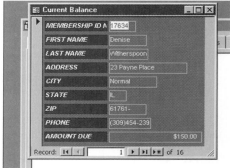

Figure 4.52
The completed Current Balance form.

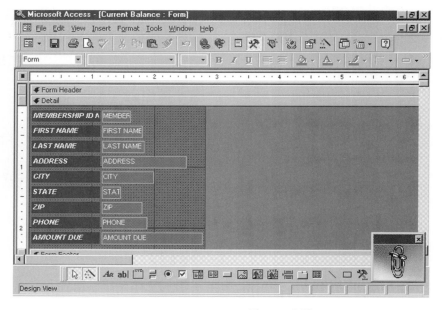

Figure 4.53
The enlarged form design window.

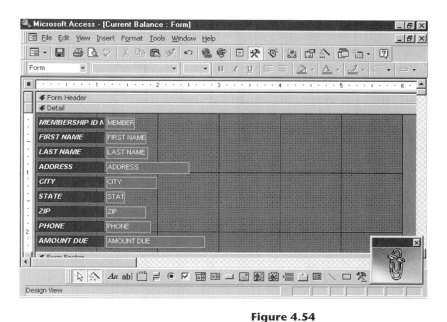

Figure 4.54
The enlarged form.

7. Enlarge the form.

Position the pointer along the right margin of the form until it becomes a horizontal resize pointer.

Click and drag   Drag the margin to the right edge of the screen. The form should look like Figure 4.54. Each field is composed of two objects: the name box and the data box.

8. Change the Membership ID Number field name to Membership ID.

Click   Click the Membership ID Number field name box. Selection handles appear around it.

Click   Click again to display all the text in the box.

Click and drag   Drag across the word *Number*.

DEL   Press to delete the text. The form should now look like Figure 4.55.

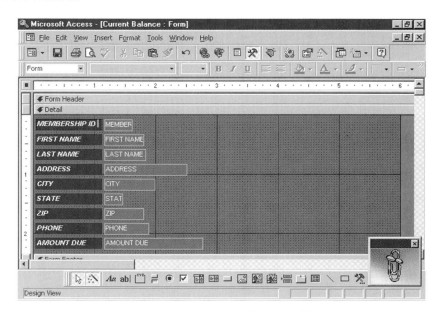

Figure 4.55
The form after the Member ID field name change.

9. **Delete the Last Name field name.**

Right-click   Right-click the Last Name field name box. The context menu shown in Figure 4.56 appears.

Cut   Click this command to delete the name box.

10. **Move the Last Name data box.**

Drag   Click and drag to move the Last Name data box to the right of the First Name data box, as shown in Figure 4.57.

11. **Repeat step 9 to delete the City, State, Zip, and Phone field name boxes.**

12. **Repeat step 10 to move the various data boxes to the locations shown in Figure 4.58.**

Figure 4.56
The Form Design context menu.

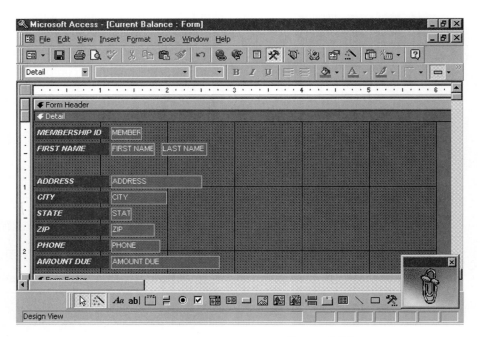

Figure 4.57
The Last Name data box moved to the right of the First Name data box.

TIMELY TIP

Be certain to delete the name box before you try to move the data box; otherwise, both boxes will move at once.

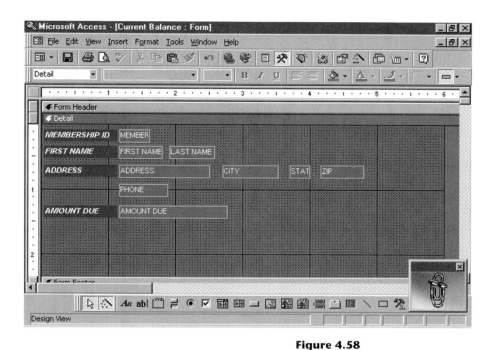

Figure 4.58
The new locations for the re-maining data boxes.

13. Test the form.

 Click to see the completed form.

 Click the Restore button of the form window to change the window size.

Drag Resize the Form window until it looks like Figure 4.59.

14. Save the changes.

 Click the Close button of the Form window. A dialog box appears, asking if you want to save the changes.

 Click to save the changes and return to the Database window.

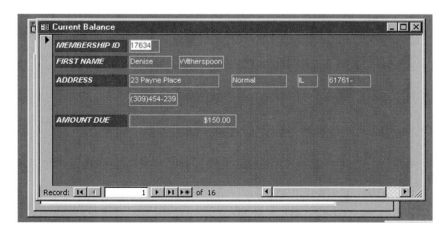

Figure 4.59
The changed form.

Reinforcing the Exercise

1. Before you can reference multiple tables in a form, they must be related to one another.
2. You can include fields from related tables in a form by using the Form Wizard.
3. Once you have defined a form, you can modify the form within the form design window.
4. Using a drag operation, you can resize the form, move fields to a new location, or increase the size of a field.
5. Access the Form Design context menu and use the Cut command to delete an entry from the form.

Adding Records to a Database Using a Form

You can use a form to enter new records, delete records, or change existing records in a database. To enter new data or to display existing data, you must activate the forms by using the Forms tab of the Database window.

Hands-On Exercise: Using a Form to Enter a New Record

Alice wants to enter a new record using the Membership Form.

1. **If necessary, open the Membership database and then open the Forms tab.**

2. **Open the form.**

Membership Form Double-click to select this form. You should see the form shown in Figure 4.60.

3. **Enter a new record.**

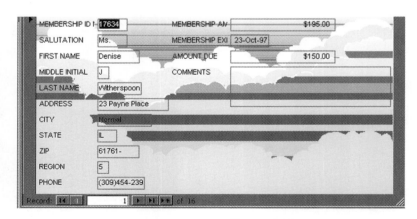

Figure 4.60
The membership form to be used for entering a new record.

Click this toolbar button to open a blank record in the form. Enter the data shown below. Be sure to press (ENTER) or (TAB) after you type the data for a field to move to the next field. There is no data for the Comments field.

Membership ID Number	33579
Salutation	Mr.
First Name	Samuel
Middle Initial	F
Last Name	Linton
Address	3462 W. Addison
City	Bloomington
State	IL
Zip	61704
Region	4
Phone	(309)663-2462
Membership Amount	125.00
Membership Expiration Date	01/03/98
Amount Due	0

4. Return to the Database window.

 Click the Close button to save the table, close the Form window, and return to the Database window.

TIMELY TIP

You may want to print your forms. To print all the forms as continuous forms, click the Print button of the toolbar. To print a certain record, position to that form and issue the File, Print command sequence. From the Print dialog box, click the Selected Records option and then print the form by clicking the OK button.

Subforms

The prior form contains data from just one table. What happens when you want to create a form dealing with two different tables, where one is the parent or master **table** and the other is the child or transaction table?

The solution is to use a **subform.** In a subform, you can add fields from a child table in a form containing a parent. This results in a one-to-many relationship. This means that several child records might appear for each parent record. Access has a **Subform/Subreport Wizard** to handle and simplify creating a subform.

Hands-On Exercise: Adding a Subform

Alice wants to be able to show the recent purchases along with membership data and the amount due (this amount does not include the recent purchases). She will modify the existing Current Balance form to accomplish this.

1. If necessary, open the Membership database and open the Forms tab.

Current Balance   Click this form.

   Click to open the form design window.

   Click to enlarge the form design window (Figure 4.61).

2. Begin the subform creation.

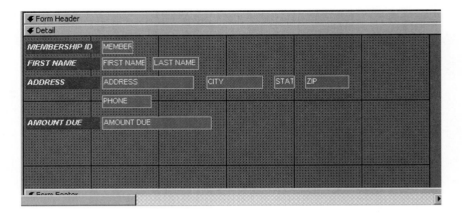

Figure 4.61
The enlarged Current Balance form design window.

   Click this toolbox button. The pointer turns into a crosshair. Move the crosshair to the 1.6-inch mark below the Amount Due field, along the left margin, and click to anchor the object box. The Subform/Subreport Wizard appears (Figure 4.62) asking where the data for the subform is located. (Make sure the Wizard button is selected.)

3. Define the subform.

   Click to accept the default of Table/Query and move to the next dialog box. This dialog box asks you to indicate the fields to be included in the subform.

4. Include the first fields from the Inventory Transactions table.

Figure 4.62
The Subform/Subreport Wizard box.

Click the down arrow in the Tables and Queries list box to see the list.

INVENTORY TRANSACTIONS

Click this table. A list of field names appears in the Available Fields list box.

MEMBERSHIP ID NUMBER

Double-click this field to include it in the Selected Fields box. This establishes the entity to link to the Membership Data table.

PRODUCT ID NUMBER

Double-click this field to include it in the Selected Fields box. This establishes the entity to link to the Inventory Data table.

5. **Include the fields from the Inventory Data table.**

 Click to open the Tables and Queries list box.

INVENTORY DATA Click this table.

ITEM Double-click this field to include it in the Selected Fields box.

PRICE Double-click this field to include it in the Selected Fields box.

6. **Include another field from the Inventory Transactions table.**

 Click to open the Tables and Queries list box.

INVENTORY TRANSACTIONS

Click this table.

UNITS Double-click this field to include it in the Selected Fields box. The dialog box should look like Figure 4.63.

7. **Define the link relationships.**

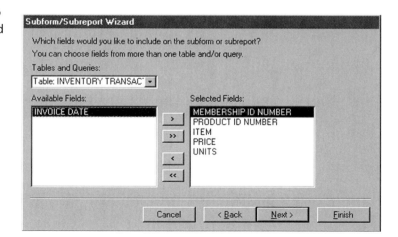

Figure 4.63
The dialog box with the fields to be included in the subform.

Next >   Click to proceed to the next dialog box (Figure 4.64). The existing links are just fine.

Next >   Click to move to the next dialog box. Access prompts you for the title of the subform (Figure 4.65).

8. **Enter the new title for the subform.**

Type: **This Period's Purchases**

Finish   The subform is now created, and the form design window appears.

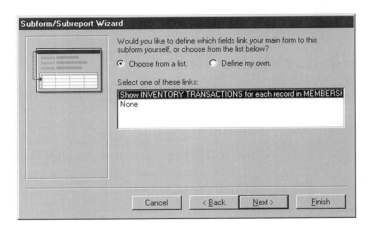

Figure 4.64
The links are established in this dialog box.

Figure 4.65
The Subform/Subreport Wizard gives you a chance to change the title.

TIMELY TIP

Depending on how you have created your form, there may not be enough room to resize the subform box. If this is the case, you first have to drag the Form Footer band downward to create more room in the Detail band of the form. Then you can increase the size of the subform box.

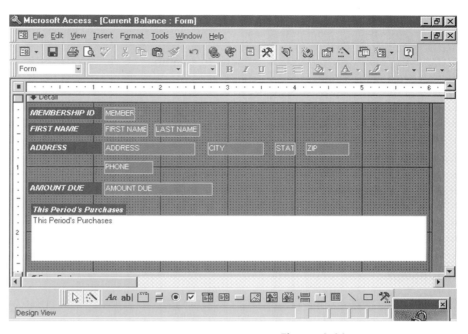

Figure 4.66
The changed form design.

Drag   If necessary, drag the subform box to the location shown in Figure 4.66.

9. **Activate the form.**

Click to see the form with the subform present (Figure 4.67). Notice that a recent purchase appears at the bot-

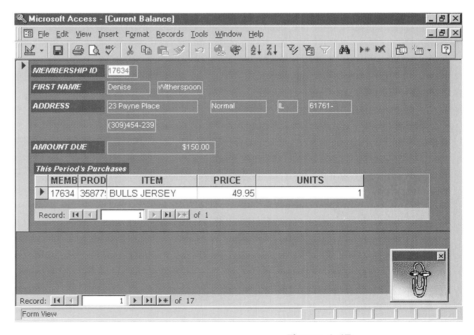

Figure 4.67
The Current Balance form with the active subform showing a recent purchase.

tom of the form. A separate speedbar for the subform also appears.

10. **Use the main form speedbar buttons to examine the various parent records.** Notice that when two child records appear, there is not enough room to display both of them.

11. **Modify the form definition.**

     Click to return to the form design window. There should be selection handles around the subform object. If there aren't, click the subform object to display the handles.

Click and drag   Click the button of the subform box on the middle selection handle, and drag downward so the form definition looks like Figure 4.68.

12. **Go back to the form and make certain that the subform is now large enough.**

13. **Save the form.**

     Click the Restore button on the Form window.

     Click the Close button. Access now asks if you want to save the changes.

     Click to save the changes and return to the Database window.

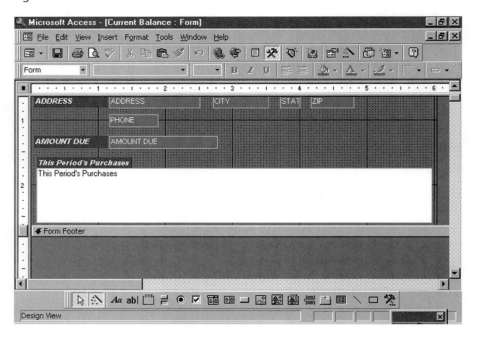

Figure 4.68
The resized subform object.

Adding Records

A benefit of creating a form with a subform is that you can use this combination form to enter data into two different tables. While this is not desirable in the above application (each form does not have all fields for a table), it is possible when you have all of the fields displayed that belong to a table.

You have probably noticed that each of the forms has its own set of form navigation buttons. To enter data for a new record in the main form, click the New Record button at the bottom of the form window. A blank form appears in the main part of the form. As you enter data in a field, you can move to the next field by pressing the Tab key. Once the record has been entered in the main form, you can click the subform's New Record button and add any data there.

Remember, as you enter information in either part of a main form or subform, you are entering data into two different tables.

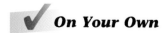

On Your Own

Using the just modified form, perform the following tasks:

- Use the Save As command to save the form to a name of your choosing.
- Use the Rectangle button of the toolbox to draw boxes around the two parts of the form to separate them visually.
- You may have to increase the size of the Detail band using a drag operation.
- Increase the size of the Form Header band using a drag operation.
- Use the Label button of the toolbox to create a label box in the Form Header band.
- Enter the heading *Member Balance and Current Purchases*.
- Change the font size of the text box to 18 pt.
- View the form and make any additional changes that you want.

Reinforcing the Exercise

1. You can use forms to enter new records in a table.
2. A subform shows multiple child records for a parent record.
3. The Subform/Subreport button of the toolbox activates the Subform/Subreport Wizard.
4. The tables you include in a subform must share a common field.
5. You can include fields from two or more tables in a subform.
6. The subform is a separate object to the form and has its own speedbar for moving through the child records.

Generating a Chart

You can use Access to build a chart that displays data graphically. You use a Form Wizard to simplify this process.

Hands-On Exercise: Building a Chart

Isabel wants to generate a pie chart showing the proportion of members in each of the cities from the Membership Data table.

1. **If necessary, activate the Membership Data table and activate the Forms tab.**

2. **Open the New Form dialog box by clicking the New button.**

3. **Indicate the type of form to be built.**

Chart Wizard   Click this option in the New Form dialog box.

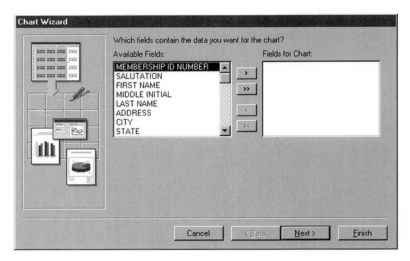

Figure 4.69
The Chart Wizard dialog box for determining the field to use in generating the chart.

      Click the down arrow button of the list box at the bottom of the New Form dialog box.

MEMBERSHIP DATA

Click this table.

OK   Click to open the first dialog box of the Chart Wizard (Figure 4.69). This dialog box prompts you for the field to be included.

City   Double-click this field name.

4. Determine the chart type.

Next >   Click to open the next dialog box, which allows you to determine the chart type (Figure 4.70).

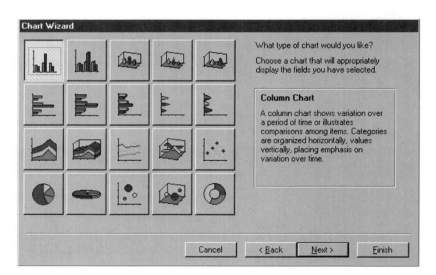

Figure 4.70
This Chart Wizard dialog box allows you to determine the chart type.

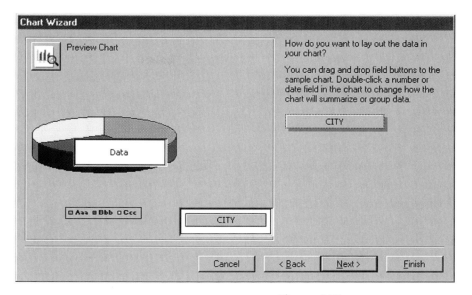

Figure 4.71
The Chart Wizard dialog box for previewing the chart.

                    Click this chart type.

5. **Preview the chart.**

> [Next >]   Click to continue to the next dialog box, which gives you
> a preview of the chart (Figure 4.71).

6. **Enter the new title for the chart form.**

> [Next >]   Click to open the Chart Wizard dialog box for changing
> the title of the chart (Figure 4.72).

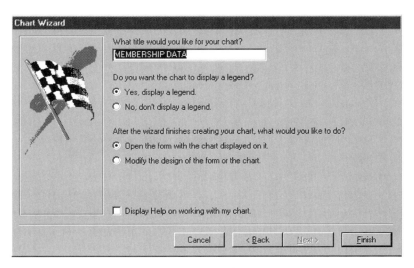

Figure 4.72
Use this Chart Wizard dialog box
to change the chart title.

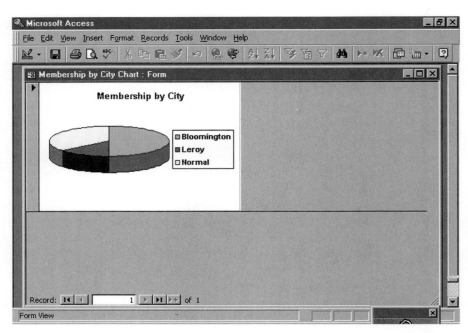

Figure 4.73
The completed chart.

Type: **Membership by City**

 Finish   Click to generate the chart (Figure 4.73).

7. **Examine the form definition.**

        Click to see the form definition in the form design win-
            dow (Figure 4.74).

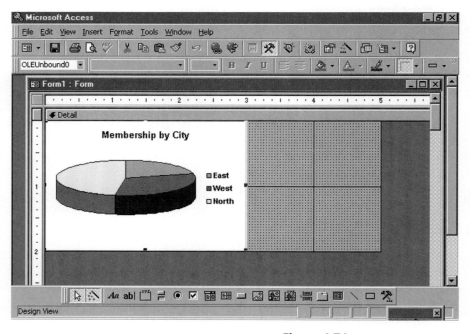

Figure 4.74
The form definition for the
chart.

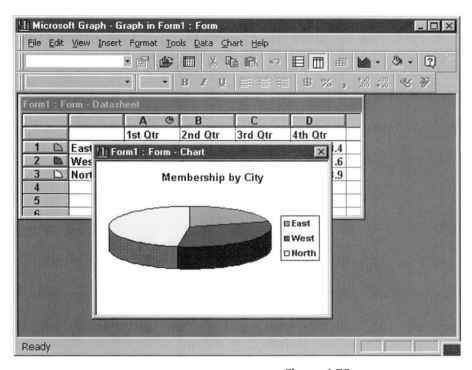

Figure 4.75
The underlying data for the chart.

8. **See the underlying data used to create the chart.**

Double-click   Position the mouse pointer over the pie chart. When
                      the pointer changes to a hand, double-click the pie
                      chart to see the underlying data (Figure 4.75). You may
                      have to move the chart to make your screen look like Fig-
                      ure 4.75.

9. **Exit the form and save.**

          Click the Close button of the Graph in Form1: Form win-
                      dow to return to the form definition window.

          Click the Close button of the form design window.

Reinforcing the Exercise

1. The New Form dialog box contains a Chart Wizard.

2. When creating a chart, you must determine the field(s) to be used and the type of chart, and enter the chart title.

3. To see the underlying data, double-click the chart in the form design window.

SESSION REVIEW

Access lets you create simple and complex queries by using Query Wizards or the query design window. Because the process of creating a query can be complicated, you should save frequently used queries so you can access them easily via the Queries tab of the Database window.

When Access executes a query, the result is displayed in a dynaset. This dynaset looks similar to the datasheet window. Only those records that match the selection criteria are displayed in the dynasheet.

Access also lets you link or relate tables that have common fields. Once you have established a link, you can display or print fields from different tables. When Access displays the fields of a query in a dynaset, you can edit any fields that are displayed or used to set up the relation. The underlying table data is automatically updated by Access.

Access lets you generate self-documenting forms that resemble paper forms. You can use these forms to input or change data via the Forms tab of the Database window.

Access provides Form Wizards that allow you to create a form with a minimum of effort. You use the Form Wizard dialog boxes to specify the tables and fields to include the type of form, the form style, and the title.

Before you can create a data entry form, you must specify one or more tables to use to tie input fields with the fields that appear onscreen. You must identify and include in the form all fields that will actively participate in the inputting or changing of data. A subform allows transaction data to be displayed with the master data for a client or customer.

The form design window automatically divides a form into three parts: the Form Header, Detail, and Form Footer bands. As you incorporate fields into the form, or as Access automatically builds the form using a Form Wizard, each field is entered as two parts. The first part is a label composed of the field name. The second part is the data box. Using selection handles, you can move both parts independently or at the same time.

In the New Form dialog box, you can choose Chart Wizard to create a graphic representation of table data.

KEY TERMS AND CONCEPTS

common field 6–120	QBE (query-by-example) grid 6–108	Sort cell 6–108
Criteria cell 6–108		SQL aggregate function 6–114
dynaset 6–102	query 6–102	subform 6–139
Field cell 6–108	Query Wizard 6–102	Subform/Subreport Wizard
form 6–125	relational operator 6–108	table 6–139
Form Wizard 6–126	Show cell 6–108	Table cell 6–108
logical operator 6–109		

SESSION QUIZ

Multiple Choice
1. Which of the following statements about an Access dynaset table is true?
   a. A dynaset is shown as read-only.
   b. A dynaset is actually a datasheet showing all records of a table.

   c. A dynaset contains fields that meet the specified criteria that can be assembled from several linked tables.
   d. None of the above statements is true.

2. A QBE grid Criteria field can be viewed by using which of the following commands?
   a. Build Expression
   b. Zoom command
   c. Edit command
   d. none of the above

3. Which of the following statements is true with respect to data entry forms?
   a. They can be more self-documenting than datasheets.
   b. They allow little control over the order in which data is entered.
   c. They do not allow automatic integration of a data screen field with a database field.
   d. None of the above statements is true.

4. Which of the following is not a valid Form Wizard?
   a. Tabular
   b. Chart
   c. Columnar
   d. Two Tables

5. The process of moving a field on a form is referred to as:
   a. moving
   b. transferring
   c. copying
   d. dragging

True/False
6. The entries that actually control how a query executes appear in the QBE grid of the query design window.

7. Linking tables requires both tables sharing one common field.

8. Only two tables can be linked using the linking capability of Access.

9. The Single-Column and Tabular Form Wizards generate the same type of form.

10. You can delete a text box used as a label for a field by selecting that control and pressing DEL.

SESSION REVIEW EXERCISES

1. A _____ is a set of instructions that specifies how Access should organize or change your data.

2. Query Wizard _____ boxes step you through the process of building a query.

3. A _____ Query built by a wizard creates a query based on questions answered in dialog boxes.

4. The results and outcome of a query are placed in a sheet called a _____ .

5. A query is controlled by entries that you or a Wizard places in the cells of the _____ grid in Design View.

6. The > symbol is an example of a _____ operator.

7. The _____ cell of the QBE grid determines the order of the records in the dynaset.

8. A Show cell contains a _____ for any field that is to appear in the dynaset.

9. The _____ cell holds relationships that determine which records will appear in the dynaset.

10. The _____ used to provide records for the query appear at the top of the query design window.

11. Click the _____ button to include a Total cell in the QBE grid.

12. _____ aggregate functions appear in the Total cell of the QBE grid.

13. The _____ command is used in a QBE Total cell to generate a total for the dynaset.

14. A _____ can be made more self-documenting than the datasheet for a table.

15. A Form _____ steps you through the process of building an Access form.

16. Once you have built a form definition, you can modify it by _____ fields to different locations.

17. A field on a form is made up of a _____ box and a _____ box.

18. Use the _____ menu to delete the name or data box of a field.

19. A _____ contains child records for the parent record displayed in a form.

20. Click the _____ button to start the Subform/Subreport Wizard.

COMPUTER EXERCISES

The Paytrans and Paymast tables will be used for these exercises. The definition of the Paymast table is shown in Figure 4.76 and the definition of the Paytrans table is shown in Figure 4.77.

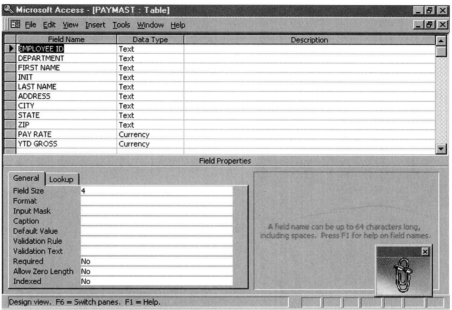

Figure 4.76
The file definition of the Paymast table.

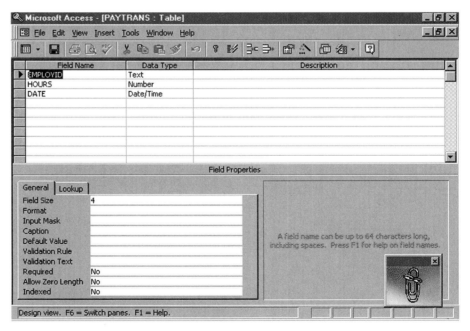

Figure 4.77
The table definition of the Paytrans table.

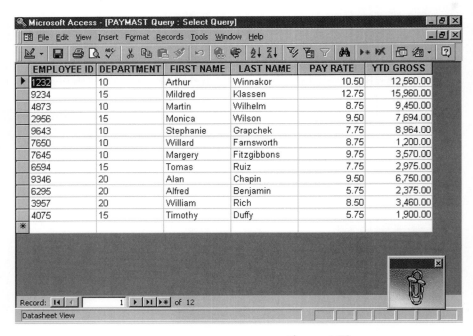

Figure 4.78
The Paymast Query dynaset to be used in queries.

1. Create a query specification that displays a dynaset like that shown in Figure 4.78. Use this specification for finding out the answers to the following queries. Be sure to print each dynaset that you generate.
   a. List employees in Department 15.
   b. List employees whose pay rate is greater than $9.00 (Pay Rate > $9.00).
   c. List employees whose year-to-date gross salary is greater than $5000 (YTD Gross > $5000).
   d. Create a query that shows the count of all employees, the grand total YTD gross, and the average YTD gross.

2. Create a query that links the Paymast and Paytrans tables so that the Hours field from the Paytrans table and the calculated Gross Pay field appears between the Pay Rate and YTD Gross columns of the dynaset. Print the dynaset.

3. Use a query table to set up the following query for the Customer Data table: Zip = 61761 and Amount > 50 or City = Bloomington.
   a. Include name and address data in the query.
   b. Print the dynaset.

4. This exercise requires the Inventory Data and Supplier Data tables.
   a. Create a query that combines the two tables using the Supplier field as the common field.
   b. Print the dynaset.

5. This exercise requires the Alumni table.
   a. Create a query that limits the records selected to those that are in the Dean's Circle.
   b. Print the dynaset.
   c. Save the query as Alumni Dean.

6. Design and create a data-entry form for your Payment table. Use the form to add two records to the Paymast table.

7. Rearrange the fields in the form created in Exercise 6 so that the form resembles the modified form that you created in the Hands-On Exercises.
    a. Save the form using a different name.
    b. Add a subform to display any child records in the Paytrans table.

INTERNET EXERCISES

1. Download a database for keeping track of addresses and other personal contact information. This requires over 1 MB of disk space.
    a. Access the Microsoft Web page with your browser (http://www.microsoft.com).
    b. Click the Products button at the top of the Web page, and then choose Access 97 for Windows 95 from the list of products.
    c. Click the Visit the Microsoft® Access 97 for Windows® 95 Website link located in the Contents bar on the left side of the screen.
    d. Click the Enhancements and Assistance link.
    e. Click the Access 97 Enhancements link on the page that appears.
    f. Click the Download button beneath the Manage Personal Information with Address Book Database link.
    g. Register with Microsoft to receive the databases, and click the Finish button when done.
    h. Click the Download link.
    i. Specify a disk location to receive the requested database.
    j. Start the database and examine the features that have been embedded in it.
    k. Print a report.

SESSION 5

Advanced Access 97 Features

After completing this session, you should be able to:

➤ Use advanced Access Report features

➤ Communicate directly with Word and Excel

➤ Generate Web-accessible Access documents

Isabel and Alice want to be able to generate reports that combine fields and contain multiple lines per record to make the reports more readable. They also want to be able to embed calculations within a report definition so that better information can be presented in a report.

Isabel wants to show Alice how to make use of the OfficeLinks button to painlessly create Word and Excel documents using information from Access tables, queries, forms, and reports. Once such a document is created, its use is limited only by the imagination of the user.

Isabel also wants to be able to put documents and information in a format that can be accessed via the Civic Arena Web site that is currently being constructed.

This session covers some advanced features of Access 97. The first topic is the Report feature's ability to print multiple lines per record as well as to include calculations in a report. The session next discusses the OfficeLinks button, which you can use to pass Access data directly to Word or Excel. The ability to convert Access tables and documents to Web documents is also covered.

ADVANCED REPORT FEATURES

The reports you have printed so far with the Report feature have been relatively simple. The advanced commands introduced in this section let you print reports with subtotals and other calculations as well as reports that format information from each record into multiple lines within a column of print.

Creating Multiple-Line Reports

In this section, you will create a multiple-line report that has the First Name and Last Name fields joined. It will also join the City, State, and Zip fields.

When you generated reports earlier in the module, the First Name and Last Name fields were separated by spaces and appeared as separate fields (columns) in the report. This format was the result of the Report feature treating the fields as two discrete pieces of data. Frequently, you will want the first name and last name to appear joined together, with only a space separating them (the common way of representing these two fields).

You can join text fields through a three-step process known as **concatenation:**

1. Use the Text Box button of the toolbox to create an unbound box in the Detail band. The unbound box consists of both a data box and a name box (Figure 5.1). You will use this unbound box to enter a **concatenation expression,** or formula.

2. Open the Properties sheet (Figure 5.2) by double-clicking the unbound data box or by right-clicking the unbound data box and then selecting Properties from the context menu. Enter the concatenation expression in the Control Source cell in the Properties sheet.

3. Change and move the field name box to reflect the contents of the expression entered in the data box. You can also just delete the name box. Figure

TIMELY TIP

The concatenation discussed here is placed in a two-part unbound control. An **unbound control** is not associated with a particular field in a table (see Figure 5.1). A control that is associated with a particular field is a **bound control**. When you use a Wizard to build a form, all the controls created are bound to their respective fields/tables.

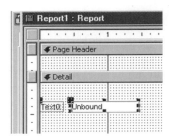

Figure 5.1
The empty unbound box for entering a concatenation expression.

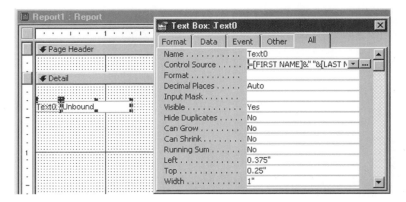

Figure 5.2
The Properties sheet for the Unbound box with the concatenation expression in the Control Source cell.

5.3 shows the name box deleted from the Detail band and a name box placed in the Page Header band. Also notice that the data box contains the concatenation expression.

Building a Concatenation Expression

You can define a concatenation expression by using the Expression Builder dialog box (Figure 5.4) or from the keyboard. To use the Expression Builder requires an extensive use of the mouse to generate various portions of the expression. In this session, you will be entering the formulas from the keyboard.

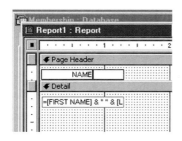

Figure 5.3
The concatenation expression moved to a different location after the field name box was deleted from the Detail band and added in the Page Header band.

An important part of the concatenation expression is the **concatenation character**—the ampersand (&). Usually fields you concatenate have extra spaces at the right end of the field because you have not filled the entire field with data. You must remove these spaces before you can join the fields. When you join a field to another field by using the concatenation character, be sure to include a space between the fields to make the data readable. For example, you would not want to see *JimBain* entered as a name. It is not only more readable but also more correct to display such data as *Jim Bain*. To concatenate the First Name and Last Name fields, you enter the following statement:

=[FIRST NAME]&" "&[LAST NAME]

Square brackets appear around the field names. You embed the space between the first name and the last name by entering a character string that consists of a space between double quotation marks (") surrounded by ampersands (&).

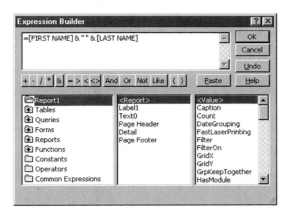

Figure 5.4
The Expression Builder dialog box for concatenating fields.

Suppose you want to report data from the Membership Data table in the format shown in Figure 5.5. The name of this report is Expiration Name and Address Report. The report will have a page header as shown. The First Name and Last Name fields will be concatenated so no extra blanks appear between them. Addresses will appear as two lines in one column (the City, State, and Zip fields will be concatenated), and the Phone, membership Expiration Date, and membership Amount fields will appear after the address field.

To build this report, you will be using the Report Wizard to enter some fields. Once you have created the report, you will enter other fields and headings manually. The Last Name field will serve as a placeholder field to avoid a lot of field movement once the report is built by the Wizards. The report will be in order by last name.

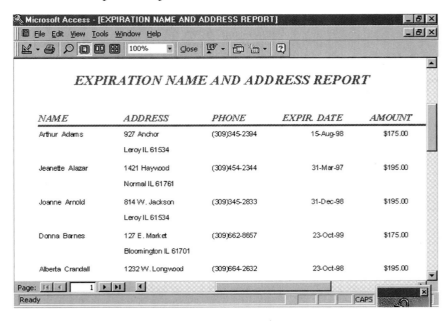

Figure 5.5
Report created from the Membership Data table by using concatenation.

Hands-On Exercise: Building the New Report Definition

Alice wants to build a report to help her keep track of membership expiration dates and amounts owed.

1. **Activate the MEMBERSHIP database.**

2. **Specify the table and type of report to be generated.**

     Click to open the Reports tab of the Database window.

     Click to open the New Report dialog box.

Report Wizard   Click this entry in the New Report dialog box.

    OK   Click to open the Report Wizard dialog box which allows you to specify the tables and fields to be included in the report (Figure 5.6).

3. **Specify the table and initial fields.**

     Click the down arrow of the Tables/Queries list box.

MEMBERSHIP DATA

    Click this table.

LAST NAME   Double-click this field name in the Available Fields list box.

ADDRESS   Double-click to include this field.

PHONE   Double-click to include this field.

MEMBERSHIP EXPIRATION DATE

    Double-click to include this field.

MEMBERSHIP AMOUNT

    Double-click to include this field. The completed dialog box should now look like Figure 5.7.

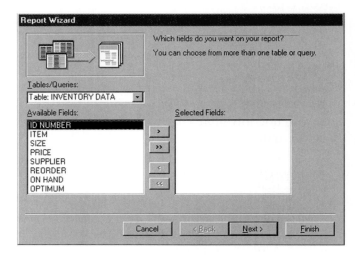

Figure 5.6
The Report Wizard dialog box, for specifying the tables and fields to be included within the report.

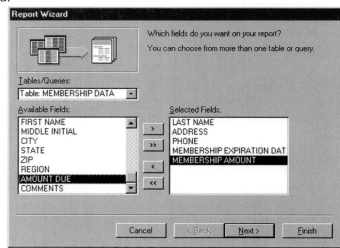

Figure 5.7
The Report Wizard dialog box with the fields to be included in the report.

4. Specify the grouping of records and the order of the report.

Next >	Click to open the Report Wizard dialog box for determining the report grouping (Figure 5.8). You don't want to group the records.
Next >	Press to specify records that will not be grouped in the report. The next dialog box opens to determine the report order.
	Click to open the list box for determining the field order.
LAST NAME	Click this field name to place the report in order by last name. The completed dialog box should look like Figure 5.9.

5. Determine the report layout.

Next >	Click to display the dialog box for determining the report layout (Figure 5.10).
Next >	Click to accept the default report layout and open the next dialog box. Access prompts you for the report style (Figure 5.11). You want to accept these suggestions.

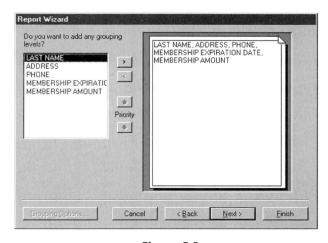

Figure 5.8
The Report Wizard dialog box for determining the record grouping within the report.

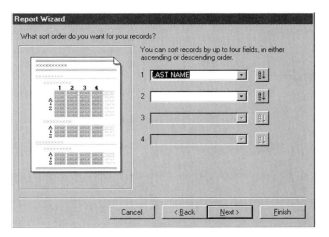

Figure 5.9
The dialog box for placing the report records in order by last name.

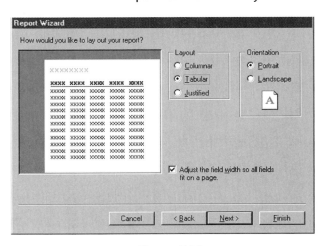

Figure 5.10
The suggested report layout offered by Access.

6. Enter the new report title.

Press to accept the default report style and proceed to the next dialog box. In this dialog box, Access gives you the option to use a report title that is different from the name of the table.

Type: **EXPIRATION NAME AND ADDRESS REPORT**

This Report Wizard dialog box should look like Figure 5.12.

7. View the report.

Click to create the report based on your specifications. When the report is finished, Access displays it in the Print Preview window.

8. Maximize the Print Preview window.

Click to maximize the Print Preview window. The screen should look like Figure 5.13. (Use the scroll bars to position in this manner.) Notice that the Phone field is not large enough. Also the date and amount fields are too large because of the long headings.

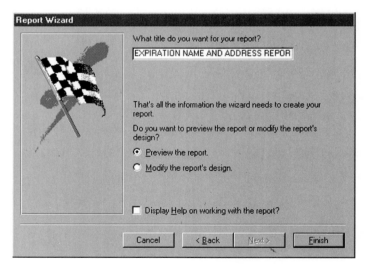

Figure 5.11
The Report Wizard suggestion for the report style.

Figure 5.12
The last dialog box of the Report Wizard contains the report title.

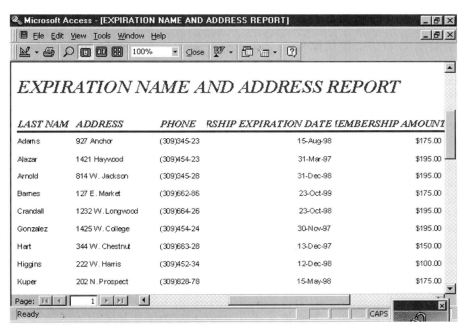

Figure 5.13
The Print Preview window for
the previewed report.

9. **View the report definition.**

Click the View button on the toolbar to open the report
design window, which shows the specifications that Access used for creating the report (Figure 5.14). If the toolbox is in the way, drag it to the bottom of the window.

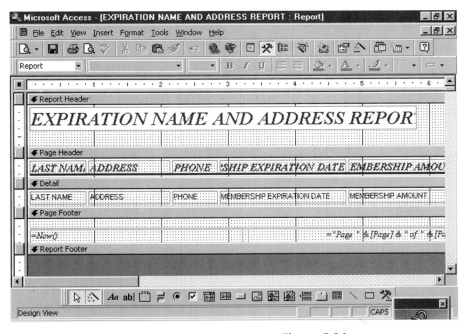

Figure 5.14
The report definition used for
creating the report.

10. Increase the size of the Detail band.

Click   Move the pointer to the top border of the Page Footer
                             band. The pointer should change into a vertical resize
                             pointer. Drag to below the Report Footer band to in-
                             crease the size of the Detail band. The Detail band should
                             now look like Figure 5.15.

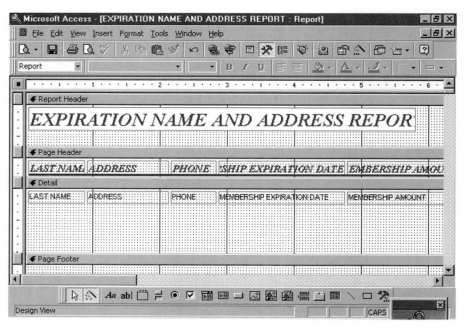

11. Change the report header.

EXPIRATION NAME AND ADDRESS REPORT

                             Click this entry. The selection handles appear.

                 Click the down arrow of the Font Size box on the toolbar.
                             It currently has the value of 20.

16   Click to change the font size to 16 points.

**12. Create the concatenation expression for the First Name and Last Name
fields.**

                 Click this button on the toolbox, point to the middle of the
                             large blank area in the Detail band, and click again. An un-
                             bound box with selection handles appears (Figure 5.16).

Right-click   Right-click the unbound data box to open the context
                             menu.

                 Click to open the Properties sheet.

Control Source   Click this cell.

Type the concatenation expression: **=[FIRST NAME]&" "&[LAST NAME]**

                 Click the Close button of the Properties sheet.

Figure 5.15
The report definition with the
enlarged Detail band.

TIMELY TIP

Make certain that you
do not include any
spaces after the closing
bracket in the concate-
nation expression. If
you do, Access will gen-
erate an error message
indicating that it can't
find the field name.
Also make certain that
you enter the leading
equal sign (=).

TIMELY TIP

Once you have created a control on the report, you can modify that control by sizing or formatting it or you can move it to a different position in the report area.

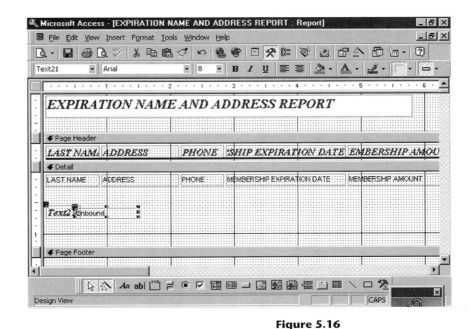

Figure 5.16
The new unbound box has been created.

LAST NAME	Right-click the Last Name field in the Detail band to open the context menu.
Cut	Click to erase the field.
Right-click	Right-click the name box of the unbound box to open the context menu.
Cut	Click to erase the name box.
Drag	Click and drag to move the new concatenation field to the location formerly occupied by the Last Name field (Figure 5.17). This field and the Address field should overlap.

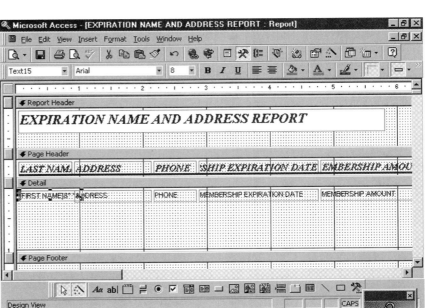

Figure 5.17
The changed Detail band.

13. **Erase part of the column heading.**

LAST NAME   Click this field name box to select it.

Drag   Click and drag to select the word LAST and the trailing space.

DEL   Click to erase that part of the field name.

14. **Shrink and move fields to the right as well as change headings.** Use Figure 5.18 as a guide for shrinking and moving the fields. Make the Phone field slightly larger when you move it. Change any headings as shown in Figure 5.18. After you have moved the other fields, make the concatenation field slightly larger.

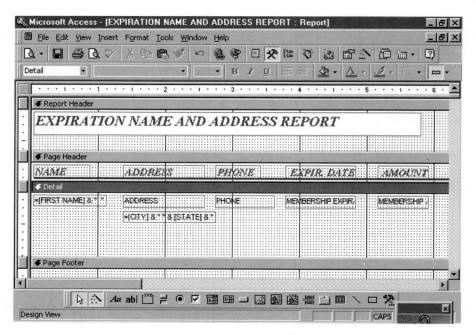

Figure 5.18
The new location for the fields and headings.

15. **Create the concatenation expression for the City, State, and Zip fields.**

      Click this button in the toolbox, point to the middle of the large blank area below the left border of the Address field, and click again. An unbound box with selection handles appears.

Right-click   Right-click the unbound data box to open a context menu.

Properties   Click to open the Properties sheet.

Control Source   Click this cell.

Type the concatenation formula: **=[CITY]&", "&[STATE]&" "&[ZIP]**

      Click the Close button of the Properties sheet.

16. Delete the name box.

Right-click   Position the pointer over the name box of the concate-
                     nated field, and right-click to open the context menu.

Cut   Click to delete the name box.

17. Reposition the concatenated field and resize it as shown in Figure 5.19.

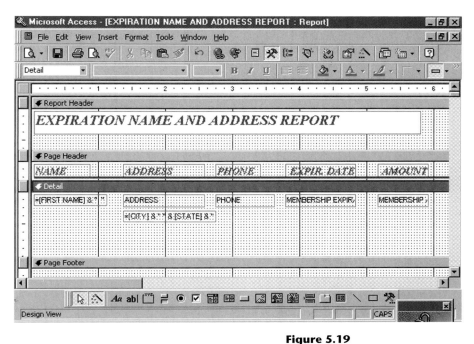

Figure 5.19
The changed and positioned box
for the concatenated field.

18. Shrink the Detail band to look like Figure 5.20.

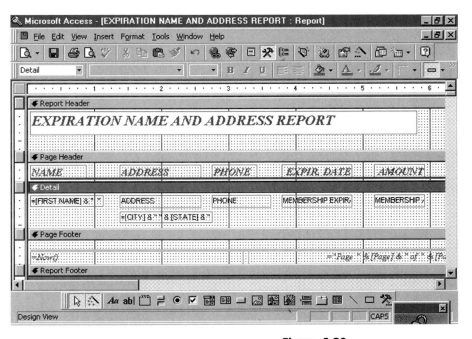

Figure 5.20
The completed Detail band.

19. Center the report heading.

Click   Click the heading to select it.

                     Click to center the heading.

20. Preview the report.

                     Click to invoke the Print Preview window. The screen
                         should look like Figure 5.21. (You may have to use the
                         scroll bars to see this portion of your report.)

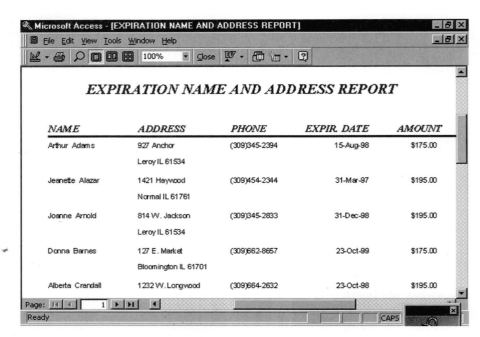

Figure 5.21
**The completed report shown in
the Print Preview window.**

21. Print the report.

                     Click to print the document.

22. Save the report.

                     Click the Close button of the Print Preview window to re-
                         turn to the report design window.

                     Click the Close button of the report design window. A di-
                         alog box appears, asking if you want to save the changes.

                     Click to save the changes and return to the Database
                         window.

TIMELY   TIP

If you inadvertently en-
ter extra blank lines in
the Detail band, you
can get rid of them by
decreasing the size of
the Detail band.

Reinforcing the Exercise

1. Fields can be joined through a process known as concatenation.
2. The Text Box button on the toolbox places an unbound box in the report design window.
3. You open the Properties sheet for an object to specify concatenation.
4. Enter the concatenation formula in the Control Source cell of the Properties sheet.
5. You can use a context menu to delete a report definition object.
6. You can move or resize fields by using a drag operation.

Embedding Calculations Within a Report Template

Besides providing subtotals of numbers falling within certain sub-groups and printing multiple lines per record, the Report feature also lets you define **calculated fields** to perform calculations as a report is printed. For instance, Access can multiply a number of inventory units in one numeric field by an item price in another numeric field to generate a value in a calculated field in the report. Calculations can also involve numeric constants or combinations of fields and constants.

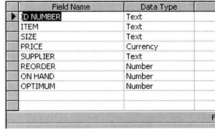

Figure 5.22
The table structure of the Inventory Data table.

To explore this feature, you will use the Inventory Data table from the Membership database to generate a report that multiplies the number in the On Hand field (the number of items) by the number in the Price field (the price per item) and shows the extension in a new field. Figure 5.22 shows the structure of the Inventory Data table. With the exception of the Price field, all numeric fields are integers to allow only whole (no fractional) unit values. The report you will generate, called Inventory Valuation Report, will look like Figure 5.23. You will, of course, use an expression to create the formula for the calculated field. The expression that you will use is:

=[PRICE]*[ON HAND]

This expression contains two fields. An expression can also have a mix of fields and numeric constants or only numeric constants.

To generate the grand total of the calculated field for all records, you use the following expression:

=sum([PRICE]*[ON HAND])

You can place this expression in the Report Footer band.

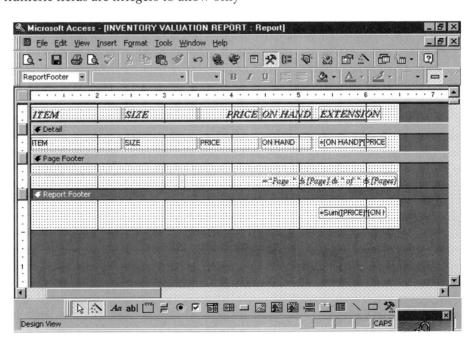

Figure 5.23
The final report you will create in this section.

Hands-On Exercise: Creating the Inventory Valuation Report

Help Alice build a report that will show the value of the gift shop's inventory.

1. **Make sure the Membership Database is open.** Begin generating the report with the Report Wizard.

Reports   If necessary, click to open the Reports tab of the Database window.

New   Click to open the New Report dialog box.

Report Wizard   Click to open the first Report Wizard dialog box, which prompts you to specify the table and fields to be included in the report.

2. **Specify the table and fields to be included in the report.**

                Click the down arrow of the list box. A listing of available tables appears.

INVENTORY DATA   Click this table.

OK   Click to open the next Report Wizard dialog box, which asks you to specify the fields to be included in the report.

ID NUMBER   Double-click this field name in the Available Fields box to include it.

Double-click   Double-click the Item, Size, Price, and On Hand fields to add them to the Selected Fields box.

OPTIMUM   Double-click to include this field as a placeholder field so that Access will reserve room for the calculated field you will be adding. The completed dialog box should look like Figure 5.24.

3. **Specify no record grouping in the report.**

Next >   Click to move to the next dialog box. Access prompts you to determine how the records in the report are to be grouped.

Next >   Click to specify no record grouping and move to the next dialog box. Access prompts you to determine how the records in the report are to be sorted.

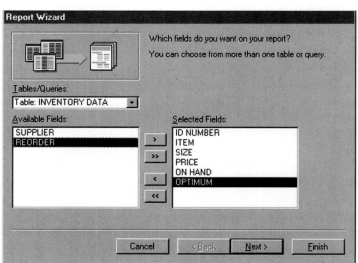

Figure 5.24
The fields to be included in the report.

4. **Specify that the report should be ordered by ID number.**

 Click to display the list of fields contained in the report.

ID NUMBER Click this field name in the Available Fields box.

Next > Click to establish the order and move to the next dialog box. Access prompts you for the report layout.

Next > Click to accept the default layout and move to the next dialog box. Access prompts you for the report style.

Next > Click to accept the default style and move to the report title dialog box.

5. **Choose a report title.**

Type: **INVENTORY VALUATION REPORT**

6. **View the report.**

Finish Click to create the report based on your specifications. The finished report is displayed in the Print Preview window.

7. **Maximize the Print Preview window.**

 Click to maximize the Print Preview window to see the generated report. The screen should look like Figure 5.25. (Use the scroll bars if necessary so your view matches the figure.)

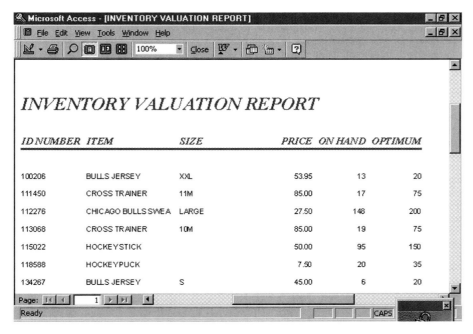

Figure 5.25
The Print Preview window displaying the report.

8. View the report design window.

 Close

Click the Close button on the toolbar. The report design window shows the specifications that Access used for creating the report (Figure 5.26).

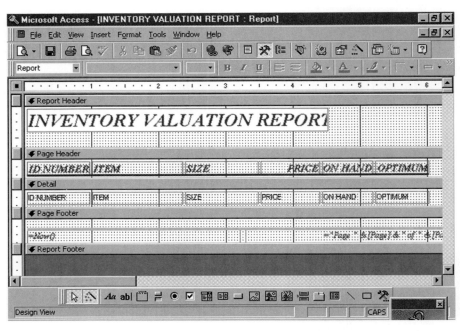

Figure 5.26
The report definition entries.

9. Delete the Optimum field name box and data box by using the context menu.

10. Create the expression for the calculated field.

ab|

Click this icon in the toolbox, point to the right of the On Hand field in the Detail band, and click. A box with a border now appears.

Right-click

Click the field name box of the new field to open the context menu.

Cut

Click to delete the field name box.

Right-click

Right-click to select the unbound data box and open the context menu.

Properties

Click to open the Properties sheet. If necessary, click the Data tab.

Control Source

Click this cell.

Type the formula for the calculated field: **=[ON HAND]*[PRICE]**

Format

Click this tab of the Properties sheet.

Click the down arrow.

Standard   Scroll down the list box until this option appears, and
                             then click it to select this format for displaying the calcu-
                             lated data.

        Click the Close button of the Properties sheet.

11. Create a column heading.

        Click this button in the toolbox. Position the pointer in
                             the area of the Page Header band above the calculated
                             field, and click to position the field name box.

Type: **EXTENSION**   Depending on how you positioned the name box, you
                             may now have to drag the box to position it properly
                             over the new column. If necessary, reposition the data
                             box. The screen should look like Figure 5.27.

12. Change the report header.

Inventory Valuation Report

                             Click this title to select it.

Drag   Drag the edge of the heading box to the right
                             (Figure 5.28).

        Click this toolbar button to center the heading.

You can use the Report Header and Report Footer areas to create custom reports.
These custom reports can include images and charts. When you expand a header
or footer band to include subreports, charts, or linked or embedded objects, you
are in effect creating custom pages. Custom pages allow you to include data as
well as summary data. If you have time, you may want to access the Help facility
and explore some of the following topics related to custom reports.

• Add subreports to a report using the subform/subreport button on the Toolbox. This activates the Subreport Wizard.

• Insert an image into a report using the Image button on the Toolbox. This activates the Insert Picture dialog box and allows you to specify a picture to be
  added to the report.

• Create a new report containing a chart using the Chart Wizard. From the Data-
  base window activate the Reports Tab, click the New button, select the Chart
  Wizard from the New Report dialog box, select the table to be used, and click
  OK to continue. Go through the various dialog boxes for the Chart Wizard.

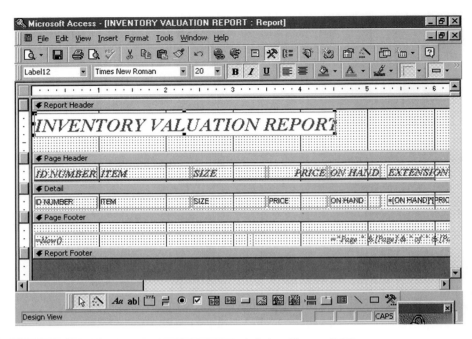

Figure 5.27
The changed Detail and Page Header bands.

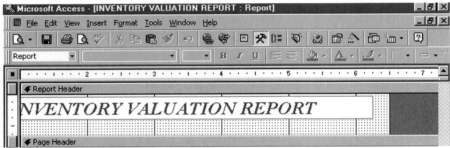

Figure 5.28
The new location of the right side of the report heading box.

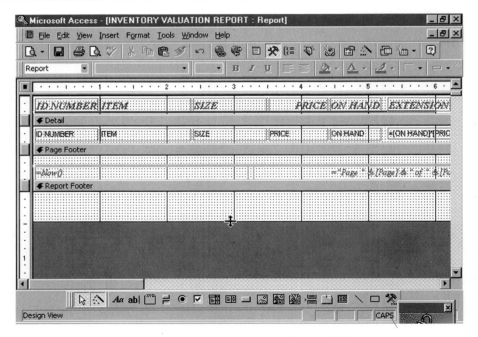

Figure 5.29
The enlarged area for the Report Footer band.

13. Expand the report footer.

Drag
Using Figure 5.29 as a guide, drag the bottom of the report footer down to create room for information.

14. Create a grand total field.

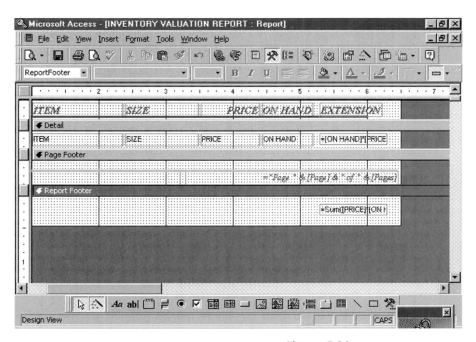

Click this icon in the toolbox, and point to and click an area below the calculated field in the Report Footer band. An unbound box with a selection border now appears.

Click to open the Properties sheet for the unbound box.

Control Source
Click this cell of the All tab.

Type the formula for calculating the grand total: **=SUM([PRICE]*[ON HAND])**
Be sure to include the parentheses.

Format
Click this cell.

Click the down arrow to open the list box.

Standard
Select this format for displaying the calculated data.

Click the Close button of the Properties sheet.

15. Delete the name box to the left of the newly created total box. The report definition should look like Figure 5.30 (move the box, if necessary).

Figure 5.30
The completed report definition.

16. Preview the report.

Click to open the Print Preview window. Scroll down until the total line appears. The report should look like Figure 5.31.

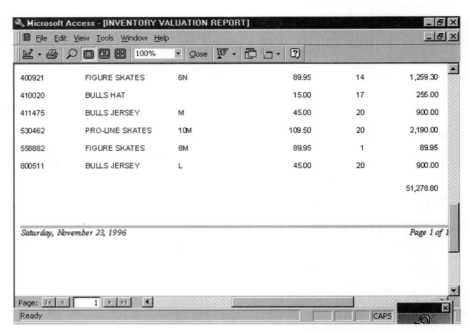

400921	FIGURE SKATES	6N		89.95	14	1,259.30
410020	BULLS HAT			15.00	17	255.00
411475	BULLS JERSEY	M		45.00	20	900.00
530462	PRO-LINE SKATES	10M		109.50	20	2,190.00
558882	FIGURE SKATES	8M		89.95	1	89.95
800511	BULLS JERSEY	L		45.00	20	900.00
						51,278.80

Saturday, November 23, 1996   *Page 1 of 1*

Figure 5.31
The finished report.

17. Print the report.

Click to print the document.

18. Save the report.

Click to return to the report design window.

Click to restore the report design window.

Click to close the window. Access asks if you want to save the changes.

Click to save the changes and return to the Database window.

Reinforcing the Exercise

1. When using the Report Wizard, you must often create a placeholder field so that Access reserves space for a calculated field.

2. Calculated fields are placed in the Control Source cell of the Properties sheet of a field data box.

3. Use the SUM function to generate a grand total of a numeric or calculated field.

4. Grand totals usually appear in the Report Footer band.

On Your Own

> Use the Chart Wizard (from the New Report dialog box) to generate a
> pie chart that shows the membership by zip code. The process will be
> similar to generating a chart from a form, as you did in Session 4.

SENDING DATA TO OTHER OFFICE APPLICATIONS

The OfficeLinks button on the toolbar allows you to quickly pass database
data to Word and Excel. You simply click an item in any one of the tabs of
the Database window and then click the OfficeLinks button.

Items from all the Database window tabs, except for the Reports tab, are
loaded into a Word document or Excel workbook as a table. A report gets
loaded into Word as a preformatted document. Once the Word or Excel
document is created, you can make changes to it, save it, and use the File,
Insert command sequence to insert it into another Word or Excel document.

When you click the OfficeLinks button, Access automatically tries to
create a Word document. If you want to create a merge file or an Excel
workbook, you must click the down arrow next to the OfficeLinks button
and then choose the desired option from the menu that appears (Figure
5.32).

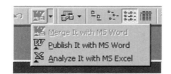

Figure 5.32
The menu that appears when
you click the down arrow next to
the OfficeLinks button.

Hands-On Exercise: Communicating with Word and Excel

Alice wants to create a table (a dynaset) containing name and address information that she can use to create Word and Excel documents.

1. **Activate the Membership database and create the query for the
   dynaset.**

   | Queries | Click to open the Queries sheet. |

   | New | Click to open the New Query dialog box. |

Simple Query Wizard   Click this entry.

   | OK | Click to open the Simple Query Wizard dialog box to de-
   termine the fields to be included in the query. |

2. From the Membership Data table, select the following fields:

First Name

Last Name

Address

City

State

Zip

Phone

Amount Due

The completed dialog box should look like Figure 5.33.

3. **Complete the dynaset.**

| Next > | Click to open the next dialog box which asks you if you want a detail or summary table (Figure 5.34). |

| Next > | Click to accept the default (Detail). The dialog box for changing the query name now appears. |

Type the name of the query: **Fields to Query**

The dialog box should look like Figure 5.35.

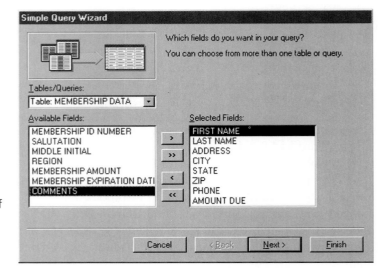

Figure 5.33
The fields to include in the query for the dynaset that will be used in linking with other Office applications.

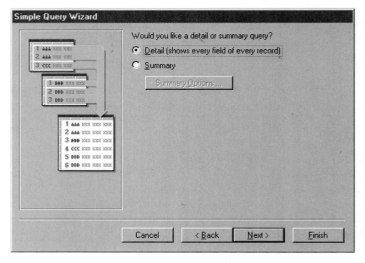

Figure 5.34
The dialog box for determining the query type.

Click to build the dynaset.

 Click to enlarge the dynaset window. The dynaset should look like Figure 5.36.

4. Close the dynaset.

 Click to make the dynaset window smaller.

Click to close the window and return to the Database window. The Queries tab should be open and the Fields to Query query highlighted.

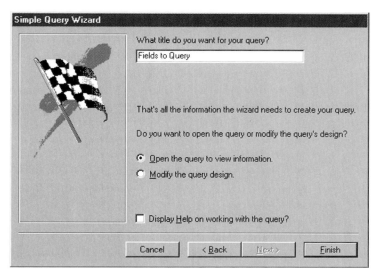

Figure 5.35
The changed title in the dialog box.

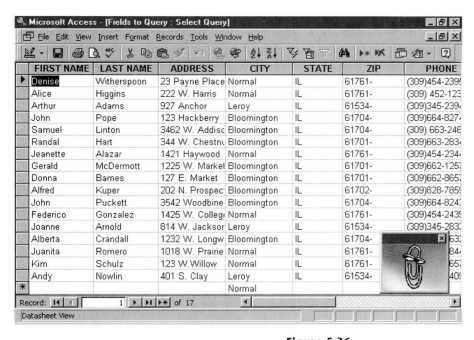

Figure 5.36
The completed dynaset.

5. Create the Word document by using the OfficeLinks button.

 Click the down arrow to the right of the OfficeLinks button. A pull-down menu opens (Figure 5.37).

Publish It with MS Word

Click to start the transfer process. After a little while, you should see the document shown in Figure 5.38. Notice that the document name in the title bar, Fields to Query, is the same as the query and that the database records have been placed in a Word table.

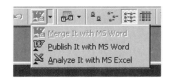

Figure 5.37
The OfficeLinks pull-down menu.

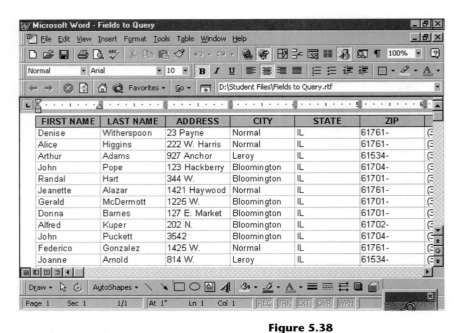

Figure 5.38
The Word document created from the Access Fields to Query dynaset.

6. **Place the document in landscape mode and print it.**

File   Click to open the File menu.

Page Setup . . .   Click to open the Page Setup dialog box.

Paper Size   Click to open this tab.

Landscape   Click to activate landscape mode.

OK   Make the changes.

7. **Verify the change.**

 Click to open the Print Preview window. The document should look like Figure 5.39.

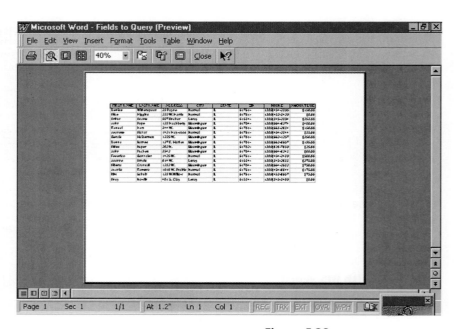

Figure 5.39
The Word document displayed in the Print Preview window in landscape mode.

Click to print the document.

 Return to the document window.

8. Close the document and save the changes.

 Click the Word Close button on the title bar. Word asks if you want to save the changes.

 Click to save the changes to the document, exit Word, and return to Access.

9. Create an Excel workbook by using the Fields to Query dynaset in Access.

 Click to open the OfficeLinks pull-down menu.

Analyze It with MS Excel

Click to start the transfer process. After a little while, you should see the workbook document shown in Figure 5.40. Notice that the workbook name in the title bar is the same as the query and that the database records have been placed in an Excel worksheet.

10. Return to Access.

 Click the Close button on the Excel title bar to return to Access.

TIMELY TIP

Before you create your first document, make certain that you have used the Open command to change the drive/directory to the location that you want to use to store your created documents. If you don't, all of the new documents will be placed in the My Documents folder.

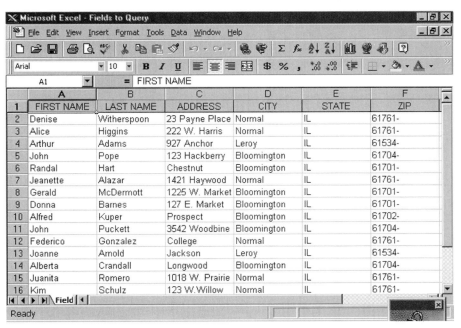

Figure 5.40
The Excel document created by the Fields to Query dynaset.

TIMELY   TIP

> Remember, once you have created a Word document using Access records, you can insert that document inside the body of another Word document using the Insert, File command sequence. You can, for example, insert an Access-created document inside the body of a report.

11. Create a Word document using a report definition.

Reports   Click to open this tab of the Database window.

Inventory Valuation Report

                         Click to select this report.

              Click to open the OfficeLinks pull-down menu.

Publish It with MS Word

                         Click to start the transfer process. After a little while, you
                         should see the document shown in Figure 5.41. Notice
                         that the document name in the title bar is the same as
                         the report.

              Click to print the document.

                         Click the Close button on the Word title bar to return to
                         Access.

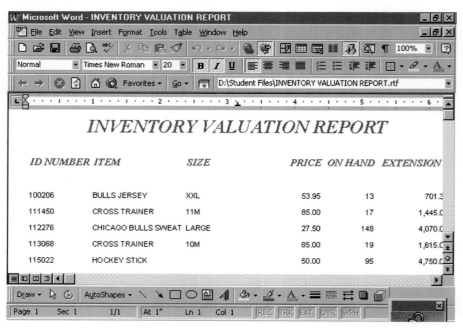

Figure 5.41
The Word document created by the Fields to Query dynaset.

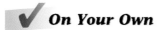
On Your Own

Use the OfficeLinks Merge It with MS Word option. (This exercise assumes you have covered Module 4, on Word 97.)

- Merge the Fields to Query table to a new document.
- Create the main document.
- Include name information.
- Make the letter an invitation to an Open House.

Reinforcing the Exercise

1. You use the OfficeLinks button to send Access data to Word or Excel.
2. Data from a table, query, form, or report can be sent to other Office applications.
3. If you send a report to Word, its report formatting goes with it.
4. When you use OfficeLinks to create a Word document, you can then insert that Word document in any other Word document.
5. You can also use OfficeLinks to merge documents in Word with Access data.

INTEGRATING DATA FROM OTHER APPLICATIONS

Access provides a number of different ways to incorporate data from other software applications in a data base. You can link and embed information as well as import information from other applications

Importing and Linking Data

When we created databases in this textbook, we entered data manually into the database. Many times when you are working with database applications you find that the data needed for your Access database already resides in a file that has been created by another piece of software. Your employer may have previously tracked information for some application using a dBASE database application for instance, or a Lotus 1-2-3 spreadsheet may contain information that you want to reside in your database. Access supports a number of data formats and allows you to import or link that data to your database.

The first decision that you have to make when getting data from another computerized source is whether to import or link the data.

When you **import** data you actually create a copy of the source data and place that copy of the original data in your Access database. You can then make any changes or perform any manipulation of the data without affecting the original data from which you made the copy. Remember that any changes that you make in your new copy do not affect the data in the original source copy.

When you **link** data you use the source data directly in your database. With a link, you do not create a new copy of the data, but rather use the original data directly.

If the data that you require is not likely to change, or if you just want a snapshot of the data, importing the data is probably the best choice. However, if the data is continually being updated in the original program or location or if having an up-to-date version is important for your application, linking may be the best alternative.

Access provides the ability to import data from these sources:

Access	Prior versions of Access databases
Microsoft FoxPro	2.x, and 3.0 (import only)
dBASE	III, III+, IV, and 5
Paradox	3.x, 4.x, and 5.0
Microsoft Excel spreadsheets	3.0, 4.0, 5.0, 7.0/95, and 8.0/97
Lotus 1-2-3 spreadsheets (link is read-only)	.wks, .wk1, .wk3, and .wk4
Delimited text files	Most files with values separated by commas, tabs, or other characters; must be in MS-DOS or Windows ANSI text format
Fixed-width text files	Most files with values arranged so that each field has a certain width; must be in MS-DOS or Windows ANSI text format

HTML files and tables

SQL tables, and data from programs and databases that support the ODBC protocol

Steps for Importing Data

Importing data into an existing database requires that you first open the database that is to receive the data (the database window is on the screen) and enter these steps:

1. Issue the File, Get External Data, Import command sequence to invoke the Import dialog box (Figure 5.42).

2. From the Files of Type selection box, select the type of data that you will be importing.

3. Locate and select the file to be imported.

4. Click the Import button.

5. Respond to any dialog boxes that might appear.

After you have imported data, that data can be used just like any other data just as if you had manually entered it in the database.

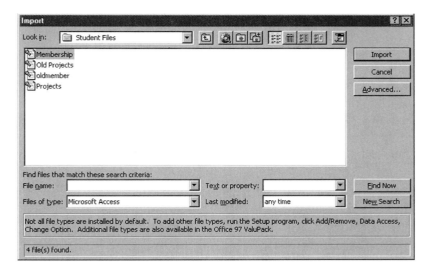

Figure 5.42
The Import dialog box used for selecting the file from which you want to import data.

Steps for Linking Data

Importing data into an existing database requires that you first open the database that is to receive the data (the database window is on the screen) and enter these steps:

1. Issue the File, Get External Data, Link Tables command sequence to invoke the Link dialog box. This dialog box looks very similar to the Import dialog shown in Figure 5.42.

2. From the Files of Type selection box, select the type of data that you will be importing.

3. Locate and select the file to be linked.

4. Click the Link button.

5. Respond to any dialog boxes that might appear.

Your use of linked data may be limited. The limitations imposed may include such things as the type of data that can be accessed, the location, and your rights (what you can do to the data). You cannot add, delete, or change the fields of a linked data table. If the original, linked data is deleted or renamed, you will not have access to that data.

Embedding Objects (Pictures)

An embedded object becomes part of the destination file and increases its size. If the object is a picture, the size of the destination file can increase dramatically. If you wish to embed pictures in a database file, the database file should always reside on some sort of high-volume storage device like a fixed disk or a zip drive.

Embedding pictures in a database table requires creating an OLE field in a table. **OLE** stands for object linking and embedding. The application in which the object is created is called the **source application**. The application that receives the object is called the **destination application**. In this case the source application is the program that was used to create the picture(s) that are to be embedded in a database table. These pictures can come in a variety of formats that can be distinguished by the file's extension: Windows Bitmap (.BMP), Encapsulated Postscript (.EPS), PC Paintbrush (.PCX), JPEG File Interchange Format (.JPG), Graphics Interchange Format (.GIF), and so forth.

Steps for Creating an OLE Field in a Table

1. Open the table in which you wish to include graphic images and invoke Design view.

2. Create a new field in the field grid and then select the OLE Object as the data type.

3. Save the changes and exit Design view.

Once you have created an OLE Object field, you can insert pictures in to that field for each record.

Steps for Inserting a Picture in an OLE Object Field

Inserting a picture in an OLE Object field is accomplished by:

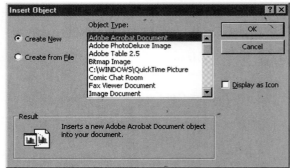

1. Selecting the OLE Object field using the Datasheet view.

2. Issue the command sequence Insert, Object to invoke the Insert Object dialog box (Figure 5.43)

3. Specify the type of object to be embedded.

4. Click the Create from File command button

5. Click the Browse button and go to the disk area that contains the file and select the file. Click the OK button to embed the file.

6. The Import Object dialog box now has the file name and location.

7. Click the OK button to embed the picture.

Figure 5.43
The Insert Object dialog box allows you to embed a picture in an OLE Object field.

Once you have embedded a picture in a field, that field contains a message indicating the type of object that occupies that field location. To view the picture/object, double-click the field to start the source application that created the image. Once the object is viewed using the application, any changes that you make become part of the embedded object.

GENERATING AN HTML DOCUMENT

Access allows you to convert any document to an HTML document that can then be accessed using a Web browser. This ability fits in well with Isabel's plans. She wants to be able to place membership expiration and renewal data as well as a merchandise catalog for the gift shop on the Civic Center's Web site. She also wants to be able to generate a control page for handling this process.

To create a Web document you use the **Publish to the Web** Wizard, which you can access by issuing the File, Save as HTML command sequence.

Hands-On Exercise: Creating Web Documents

Alice and Isabel want to generate a new report and then convert it and another report to HTML format. They also need to create a home page that will control links to other Web pages.

1. **If necessary, Open the Membership database.** Activate the Reports tab of the Database window.

2. **Build a new report using the Report Wizard.**

 — Click to open the New Report dialog box.

Report Wizard — Click to indicate that you want Wizard help.

 — Click the down arrow of the Choose the table or query box. A list of table names now appears.

Inventory Data — Click this table name.

OK — Click to open the first Report Wizard dialog box for selecting fields to include in the report.

ID NUMBER — Double-click to include this field in the report. Also include the Item, Size, and Price fields. The completed dialog box should look like Figure 5.44.

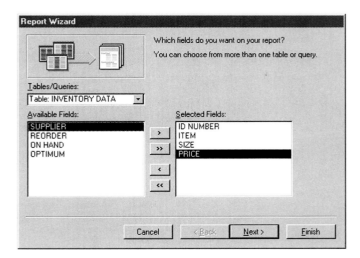

Figure 5.44
The fields to be included in the new report.

Next > — Click to proceed to the next dialog box.

Next > — Click the Next button in the next four dialog boxes until the report name dialog box appears.

Type the name of the report: **Merchandise Catalog**

Finish	Click to generate the report shown in Figure 5.45.

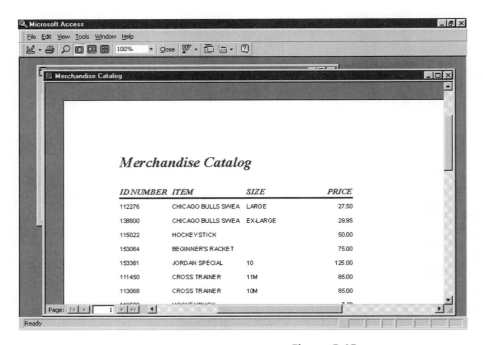

Figure 5.45
The completed Merchandise Catalog report.

	Click the Close button of the Report window to return to the Database window.

3. **Generate the HTML documents, and create the controlling home page.** Make certain that the report just created is selected.

File	Click to open the File menu.
Save as HTML	Click to open the Publish to the Web Wizard. The first dialog box appears as shown in Figure 5.46.
Next >	Click to open the next dialog box (Figure 5.47). This dialog box allows you to determine what is to be converted to HTML format. Notice the available tabs.
Reports	Click the Reports tab.

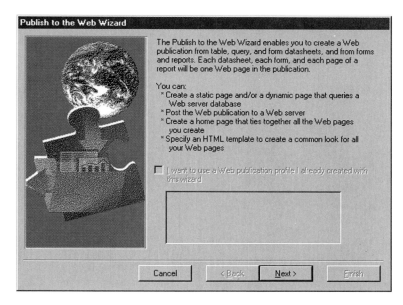

Figure 5.46
The first dialog box of the Publish to the Web Wizard.

EXPIRATION NAME AND ADDRESS REPORT

Click to include this report.

MEMBERSHIP NAME AND ADDRESS REPORT

Click to include this report.

Merchandise Catalog Click to include this report. The completed dialog box should look like Figure 5.48.

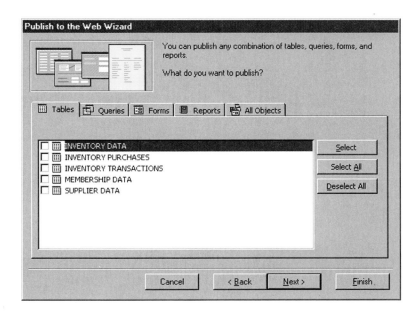

Figure 5.47
The second Publish to Web Wizard dialog box allows you to determine what is to be converted.

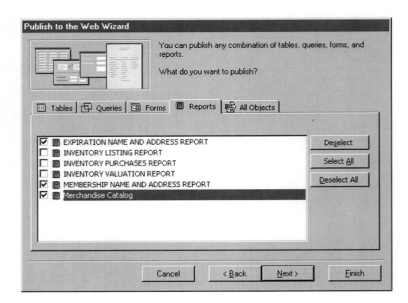

Figure 5.48
The reports selected to be converted to HTML format.

Next >   Click to proceed to the next dialog box, in which you indicate the template to be used to generate the background for the Web pages.

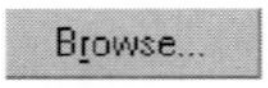

Browse...   Click this button to access the Select an HTML Template dialog box (Figure 5.49). This dialog box allows you to select the background for the HTML documents.

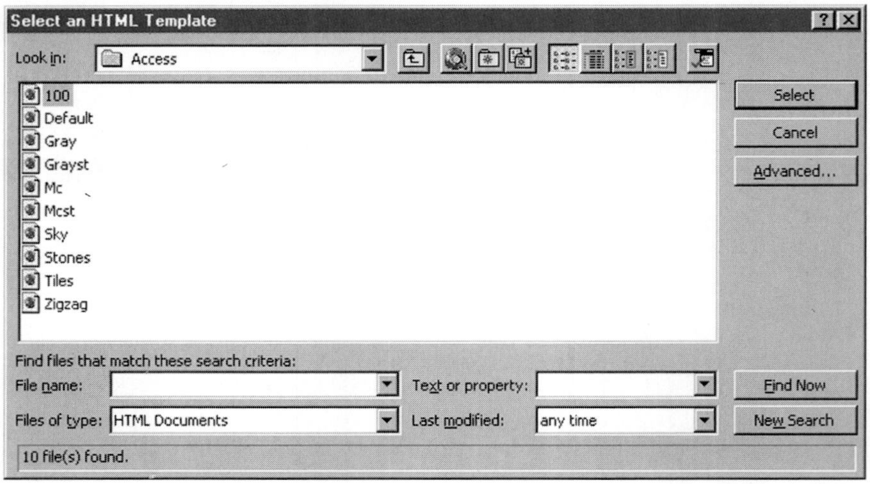

Figure 5.49
The Select an HTML Template dialog box.

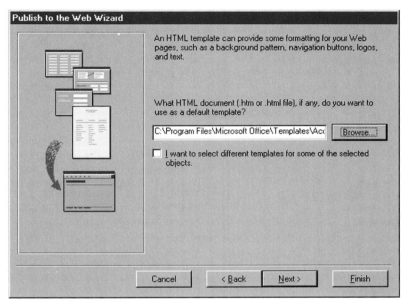

Figure 5.50
The Publish to the Web Wizard dialog box for controlling the appearance of the Web pages.

Grayst

Double-click this template to select it and return to the previous dialog box. This dialog box should now look like Figure 5.50.

Click to proceed to the next dialog box (Figure 5.51). This dialog box allows you to determine the type of HTML document you want to generate.

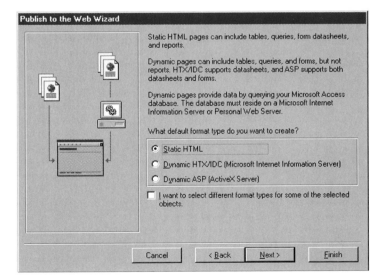

Figure 5.51
The dialog box for determining the type of HTML document to generate.

| Next > | Click to accept the default setting (Static HTML) and proceed to the dialog box that tells Access where the documents are to be stored (Figure 5.52). If necessary, change the setting to the correct location. |

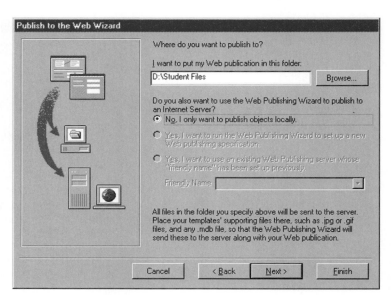

| Next > | Click to open the next dialog box, which asks if you want a controlling home page to be created. |

Yes, I want to create a home page

Click to indicate that you want a home page to be created.

Default   Click the text box that currently displays *Default*.

Type the name of the home page Web file: **Civic Center Information Page**

The completed dialog box should look like Figure 5.53.

| Next > | Click to open the next dialog box, which asks you about saving answers to a Web profile (Figure 5.54). |

| Finish | Click to accept the default setting and begin building the Web documents. |

Figure 5.52
The dialog box for determining the location to receive the converted HTML files.

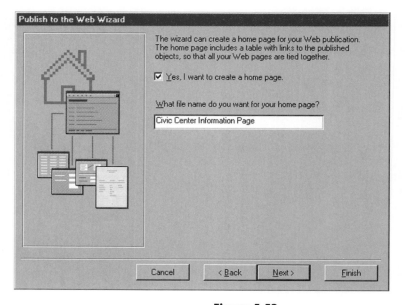

Figure 5.53
The Publish to the Web Wizard dialog box prompting you about creating a home page.

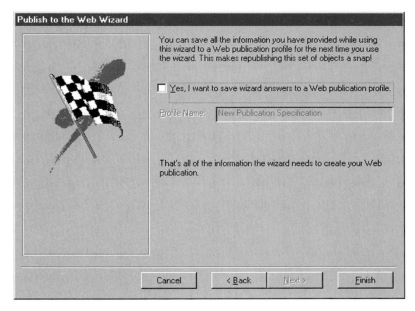

Figure 5.54
The Wizard dialog box prompting about saving a Web profile.

4. **Close all windows and exit Access.**

5. **Start Microsoft's Internet Explorer.**

6. **Change to the location of your student files on disk.**

Civic Center Information Page

Double-click this document to display the home page (Figure 5.55).

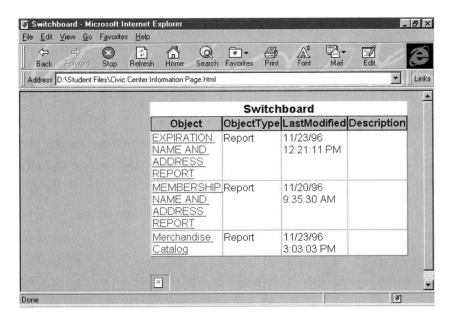

Figure 5.55
The Civic Center Information Page controls access to the other Web documents.

Merchandise Catalog

Click this link. The Merchandise catalog page appears as shown in Figure 5.56.

Click this toolbar button to go back to the home page. Examine the other pages you created.

7. **Exit Microsoft Internet Explorer.**

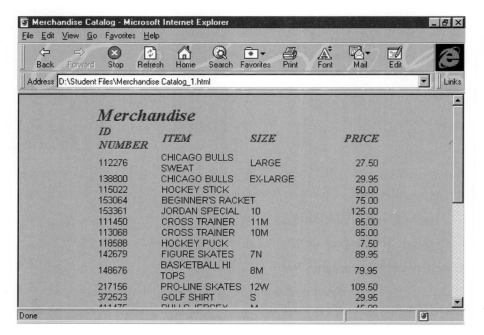

Figure 5.56
The Merchandise Catalog Web page.

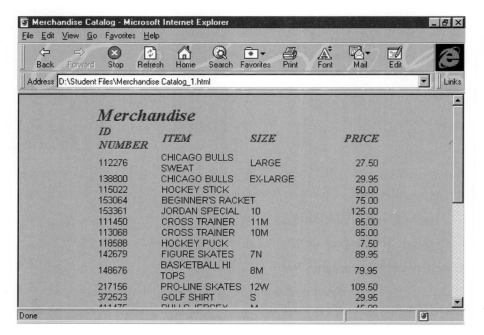

Reinforcing the Exercise

1. You can convert any information from a database to an HTML document that you can then access by using a Web browser.
2. Use the File, Save as HTML command sequence to open the Publish to the Web Wizard.
3. The Publish to the Web Wizard allows you to determine which database objects are to be converted to HTML, the type of background to be used, the type of HTML document to be created, where the documents are to reside, whether a controlling home page is to be created, and whether a Web profile is to be created.

SESSION REVIEW

Based on how the Report Wizards build reports, it appears to a beginning Access user that multiple lines cannot be generated per record. Wizards also do not provide the ability to create fields that are the result of calculations performed using data from fields. Once you have a basic report generated by using a Report Wizard, you can add these features to the report. This saves you a lot of time because you can start with an existing report design and add enhancements in the report design window.

The Properties sheet is an important Access tool for controlling objects. Access maintains a Properties sheet for any object created. An object can be a band report, a name box, a data box, and so forth. You use Properties sheets to place concatenation expressions and formulas in reports.

Although it might appear that Access allows you to print only one line per record, lines can be added to the Detail band to generate multiple lines per record. Joining fields requires using the concatenation character (&) and placing a space or any needed punctuation between fields. This is accomplished by setting up a relationship in the Expression Builder dialog box or by entering a concatenation expression in a Properties sheet.

The OfficeLinks button allows you to instantly pass information from Access to Word or Excel. You can also merge documents in Word by using OfficeLinks.

The Publish to the Web Wizard converts any database object to HTML format for placement on the World Wide Web. Once converted, these documents can be viewed using any Web browser, such as Internet Explorer.

KEY TERMS AND CONCEPTS

calculated field   6–169
concatenation   6–158
concatenation character 6–159
concatenation expression
   6–158

destination application
   6–185
importing data   6–183
linking data   6–184

OLE   6–185
Publish to the
   Web Wizard   6–186
source application   6–185

SESSION QUIZ

Multiple Choice

1. Which of the following statements is true about forcing multiple lines to appear within a data column?
   a. The semicolon (;) must be placed where each line is to end within a column.
   b. Both the + and the ; may be required.
   c. Only the colon is needed to indicate the end of a line.
   d. Full-screen editing places each heading on a separate line.
   e. None of the above statements is true.

2. Which of the following characters concatenates fields?
   a. &
   b. :
   c. ;
   d. +
   e. none of the above

3. Which of the following items is not provided for by the Publish to the Web Wizard?
   a. the background image to use
   b. where the HTML files are to be placed

c. specific pictures to include at the beginning of an HTML file

d. All of the above are provided.

4. The Control Source cell of the Properties sheet, when used to control concatenation, can be changed by:

   a. the Concatenation Builder

   b. entering the formula directly in a formula cell in the Detail band

   c. entering an expression in the Control Source cell of the Properties sheet

   d. none of the above

5. A formula is placed in a _____ box by Access.

   a. name

   b. formula

   c. data

   d. field

   e. none of the above

True/False

6. The $ deletes blanks on the left side of a field.

7. A maximum of two lines can be printed per specified field using the Report feature.

8. The Link Application button allows you to quickly pass Access information to Word.

9. Only Word can receive Access data.

10. Arithmetic statements in a report template can contain only field names.

SESSION REVIEW EXERCISES

1. Define or describe the function of each of the following:

   a. concatenation

   b. OfficeLinks button

2. More than one printed _____ can be generated for any database record in a report.

3. Joining fields together is called _____ .

4. The concatenation character is _____ .

5. Concatenation is accomplished by opening the _____ sheet.

6. The concatenation expression is placed in the _____ cell of the Properties sheet.

7. Click the _____ _____ of the toolbox to create an unbound box.

8. Click the right mouse button to open the _____ menu, which includes a command you can use to delete a report object.

9. Including a space between two concatenated fields requires entering the character string _____ .

10. A field's size can be increased using a _____ operation.

11. Specifying two fields involved in some type of arithmetic operation is called a report _____ .

12. A calculated field can include fields or _____ _____ .

13. When specifying a concatenation or calculation, field names are placed inside _____ .

14. A _____ field is inserted in a report to hold the result of a calculation.

15. A calculation is defined in the _____ _____ cell in the Properties sheet for a field.

16. When using a Report Wizard to create a report, you sometimes need to insert a _____ field to reserve room for a calculated field.

17. Use the _____ function to generate grand totals of numeric or calculated fields.

18. The _____ button allows you to send database data directly to Word or Excel.

19. The information from the _____ , _____ , _____ , or _____ Database window tabs can be used to send information to Word.

20. Information sent to Word from the _____ tab is sent as preformatted data.

COMPUTER EXERCISES

1. Perform the following tasks using the Paymast table.
   a. Create a multiple-line report. Design the report layout yourself.
   b. Generate a Groups/Totals report on total pay by department.

2. This record-keeping project deals with tracking donations that have been made to a college or university foundation. A foundation office is extremely important for providing needed funds to a school. The efforts put forth by the foundation office generate the funds for construction, faculty travel, research, and equipment.

   When people donate money to an institution, it is critical that the organization receiving the money record each donation and generate a timely thank you letter. Recording the donation properly is important because it allows the institution to keep track of individual donors and retrieve information about those donors when needed. For example, you may be interested in all individuals who have made donations of more than $1000 during the past five years. Another point that may interest you is the geographic location of donors. An efficiently built record-keeping system lets you quickly and easily answer these types of questions.

   This exercise requires use of the Alumni table provided on your Student Data Disk. Let's examine some of the fields. The Salut field contains room for just about any salutation you wish to use in a letter, depending on the individual(s) giving the gift. The salutation might be "Dear Mr. and Mrs.," "Dr. and Ms.," "Ms.," or any variation. This field is especially useful when generating letters for donors.

   The First Name, Middle, and Last Name fields are used to record the name of the principal donor. The Spouse First and Spouse Middle fields are used to record the name of the spouse, if any, who should be included in recording the donation.

   The Gift Type field is used to classify the gift. The three classifications are determined by the size of the gift:

- $1–499 = Regular (R)
- $500–999 = Dean's Circle (D)
- $1,000 and up = President's Club (P)

The Date field contains the date the gift was received, and the Amount field records the size of the gift.

a. Design, create, and print a report called Gift Edit, which contains information about each gift. This report allows manual comparison of each printed record about each gift with the original document to ensure that all gifts and the information about each were recorded properly. If any errors are detected, they are corrected immediately.

b. The report should generate more than one line per contributor. Concatenate these fields:

First and Spouse First

City, State, and Zip,

Gift Type—leave as is

c. Use the OfficeLink merge option to define a merge. Design your own thank you letter and send each contributor a personalized letter using the merge capability of Word.

3. Pass to Word an Access report that you created previously.

4. Use the Paymast table to create an Excel workbook.

5. Create a Web document using selected objects from your database. You decide on what is to be included. Use at least one table and one report.

INTERNET EXERCISES

1. Examining common questions about Access.
   a. Access the Microsoft Web page with your browser (http://www.microsoft.com).
   b. Click the Products button at the top of the Web page, and then choose Access 97 for Windows 95 from the list of products.
   c. Click the Common Questions link in the Contents bar on the left side of the screen.
   d. Examine the list of questions.
   e. Click one of the question links and print the answer that appears.

ACME INDUSTRIAL COMPANY
Subsidiary of Jergens, Inc.

Precision 'No-Counterbore' Bushings
–Quality Products Since 1912–

DANVILLE, VA. 24543
P.O. BOX 3445
804-793-0155
800-552-9120 VA.
800-446-9110 AREA

ARDEN, N.C. 28704
P.O. BOX 370
704-684-9844
800-222-3514 N.C.
800-438-0697

SANFORD, N.C. 27330
P.O. BOX 1348
919-775-7255
800-672-3559 N.C.

VIRGINIA CAROLINA TOOLS, INC.

EASLEY, S.C. 29640
P.O. BOX 1529
803-269-0232
800-922-6274 S.C.
800-654-5246

COLUMBIA, S.C. 29169
P.O. BOX 3488
803-791-8691
800-922-0665 S.C.

Cutting Tools
Tooling Components
Die & Mold Supplies
Screw Machine Supplies

Notes

Notes

Notes

Notes

Notes

Notes

Notes

Notes

OPERATIONS REFERENCE

FILE

BUTTON	MENU OPTION	KEYS	ACTION
	New Database	ALT + **F, N**	Opens a new database.
	Open Database	ALT + **F, O**	Opens an existing database.
	Save	ALT + **F, S**	Saves a database that has been previously named and saved.
	Print	ALT + **F, P**	Prints a database.
	Print Preview	ALT + **F, V**	Displays the database as it will appear when printed.
	Page Setup	ALT + **F, U**	Controls how the datasheet is laid out.

EDIT

BUTTON	MENU OPTION	KEYS	ACTION
	Cut	CTRL + **X**	Cuts selected portions of a database.
	Copy	CTRL + **C**	Copies selected portions of a database.
	Find	CTRL + **F**	Searches database for specified record.
	Paste	CTRL + **V**	Pastes cut or copied portions of a database in a new location.
	Undo	CTRL + **Z**	Reverses the last command issued.

FORMAT

BUTTON	MENU OPTION	KEYS	ACTION
	Cells	(ALT) + **O, E**	Changes the format of cells, such as the appearance of gridlines.
	Hide Columns	(ALT) + **O, H**	Hides columns so they are not displayed or printed.
	Unhide Columns	(ALT) + **O, U**	Redisplays columns that have been hidden.
	Column Width	(ALT) + **O, C**	Changes the width of columns.

RECORDS

BUTTON	MENU OPTION	KEYS	ACTION
	Filter, Advanced Filter/Sort	(ALT) + **R, F, A**	Rearranges records according to values contained in multiple specified fields
(A/Z↓)			Rearranges records in ascending order according to the value of one specified field.
(filter icon)			Performs a sort.
(filter grid icon)			Displays only specified fields.
(▶*)			Creates a new record in a database.

TOOLS

BUTTON	MENU OPTION	KEYS	ACTION
	Relationships	(ALT) + **T, R**	Links two tables in a database.

GLOSSARY

AutoNumber field A field that allows you to number the records as they appear in a table, query, and so forth. Cannot be updated.

calculated field A field you can add to a report template to perform a calculation as the report is printed.

child table The table related to the parent table. Often has several records for each record in the parent table.

concatenation A three-step process of joining text fields.

concatenation character The ampersand (&) used in the concatenation expression to join text fields.

concatenation expression Expression used to join text fields and entered in an unbound box in the Detail band.

Criteria cell Portion of the query design window in which you enter any selection criteria for including records in the dynaset for a specified field.

Currency field Holds money-related data to be used in calculations.

database A set of information related to a specific application. Can be viewed as a large repository (like a file cabinet) in which tables, reports, queries, and other objects are stored.

Database window Shows all tables related to the activated database. Tabs along the top of the window represent different types of objects related to the open database.

Datasheet window Used to display a table for which you have created a structure and to add or edit data in a table.

data type Determines the type of field in a database.

Date/Time field Contains eight positions and automatically has the slashes (/) in the correct locations.

Design View The view that a report appears in when you are creating it. In this view, the report is divided into bands.

Detail band In the Design View of a report, contains the actual data from the database table.

dynaset A display of a newly created query. Contains the fields you specified in the query and provides a view of data contained in the database tables you specified. You can work with data in a dynaset just as you do in a table, except in a dynaset, you can work with several fields from several different tables. Any changes you make to the fields in a dynaset are automatically included in the records of the underlying tables.

expression builder Used to enter a validation rule.

field A unit within a record that contains a fact about the entity.

Field cell Area of the query design window where the names of the fields to be included in the query are specified.

Field Properties box Controls the length, alignment, fill characters, color, and other features of a field.

filter Used in a sort operation to process the data and rearrange it in the table based on a selected field.

form A customized data entry form that is similar to a source document. Allows you to include more text to make the form self-documenting.

Form Wizard A feature that steps you through the process of creating a form.

gridlines The lines that appear around each cell of a table displayed in the Datasheet window.

Group Footer band In the Design View of a report, contains any identifying text and subtotals that have been generated for a group of records.

Group Header band In the Design View of a report, contains information such as a group name or text that you want to print at the beginning of a group of records.

importing data Getting data from another computerized source; linking the data.

input mask Specifies how data is entered and displayed in a table.

input mask characters Characters you can enter in the Input Mask cell of the Field

Properties box to control how data is entered and displayed in a table.

Input Mask Wizard   A feature that steps you through the process of building an input mask.

key   A designated field used to order, identify, or retrieve records in a database.

linking data   Using source data (original data from another computerized source) directly rather than creating a copy of the data.

logical operator   Operators such as And, Or, and Not used to link fields when a query requires examining several fields.

many-to-many relationship   A relationship between tables in which several parent records have matching keys in the child, and several child records have matching keys in the parent.

Memo field   Holds large documents (up to 64,000 bytes or characters of data).

menu-driven   One of the modes Access runs in. This easy-to-use interface lets you issue commands without an in-depth understanding of Access.

Number field   Restricted to the plus or minus sign, numerals, and the decimal point. You must use this data type anytime you want to perform calculations.

OLE object field   Stores objects from other Windows applications that support object linking and embedding.

one-to-many relationship   A relationship between tables in which several child records exist for each parent record. This is the most common type of relationship.

one-to-one relationship   A relationship between tables in which one child record exists for each parent record. This type of relationship is rarely seen in the real world.

orphan record   A child record with no related parent record.

Page Footer band   In the Design View of a report, contains the text or data that are placed at the bottom of each page of the report.

Page Header band   In the Design View of a report, defines the area at the top of each page of the report. Contains such information as page numbers, dates, and titles.

parent table   The table used as the main table for a relationship. The record pointer in the parent table controls how records are accessed in the child table.

permanent link   A link established between two tables by using the Relationships command. A permanent link is always in effect after it has been defined.

primary key   The unique identifier for a particular record, most often a customer number or Social Security number. When a database is in primary-key order, the records can appear in the table in order by the contents of the field used to build the primary key, but no two records can have the same key value.

Program mode   One of the modes Access runs in. Allows you to store instructions in a Visual Basic program file and execute all of them with one command.

Properties sheet   Shows the rules governing how a section or object is displayed.

Publish to the Web Wizard   A feature that takes you through the steps of creating a Web document.

QBE (query-by-example) grid   Appears at the bottom of the query design window and used to control which fields are to appear in the dynaset, how fields are to be sorted, whether or not a field is to be displayed, and any criteria to use in including fields in the dynaset.

query   A set of instructions that specifies how Access should organize or change your data.

Query Wizard   A feature that takes you through the steps of creating a query.

record   A unit within a table. Each record in a table contains related information about an entity.

record pointer   A right arrow that appears in the left margin of the Datasheet window and helps you keep track of where you are within a table. The record number that appears in the speedbar is the current location of the record pointer.

referential integrity   Requires that every child record be related to a parent record.

relational database   A database that allows you to link records from two or more tables based on the contents of a common field.

relational operator   Operators such as < (less than), > (greater than), and = (equal) used in the selection criteria you enter in the Criteria cell of the query design window.

report   A printout of records in a database.

Report Footer band   In the Design View of a report, contains text and data that you want to print at the bottom of the last page of a report, such as a grand total figure.

Report Header band   In the Design View of a report, contains information that you want to appear only on the first page of the report.

report template   Contains the format, headings, and fields to be included in a report. You can create a report template by using the Report Wizard or you can design it yourself.

Report Wizard   A feature that steps you through the process of building a report.

secondary key   Used to arrange a database in an order other than the primary-key order. Allows multiple occurrences of the same value.

Show cell   Portion of the query design window used to determine whether or not a field is to be displayed in the dynaset.

Sort cell   Portion of the query design window that displays a list box with the options Ascending, Descending, and (not sorted). Allows you to determine the order that fields appear in the dynaset.

speedbar   Appears at the bottom of the Datasheet window. Contains several navigation buttons and displays the record in which the pointer is currently located and how many records are in the entire table.

SQL aggregate function   Functions such as Group By, Sum, and Avg used in a query against groups of records.

subform   Used to create a form that contains data from two different tables.

Subform/Subreport Wizard   A feature that steps you through the process of creating a subform.

table   The storage entity for a database. A table is made up of records that contain data about a single thing, such as a person or a sales transaction.

Table cell   Portion of the query design window where the name of the table from which the field is obtained is specified.

table structure   A set of instructions regarding the arrangement of information within each record, the type of characters (numeric or alphanumeric, for example) used to store each field, and the number of characters required by each field.

Text field   Holds any alphanumeric character (number, letter, or special character).

toolbox   A floating palette that is displayed whenever you open the Design View of a report.

transient link   A link between two records that is defined by using the query-by-example feature of Access. A transient link is temporary.

validation rule   An algebraic or logical expression that Access evaluates when data is entered in a field.

validation text   Text that appears in an alert dialog box if the data entered in a field does not conform to the expression entered in the validation rule.

Yes/No field   Contains Y (yes) or N (no) and is thus always only one position in length.

INDEX